SCALE MILITARY
FIGURE CONVERSIONS

SCALE MILITARY FIGURE CONVERSIONS

DUNCAN HOWARTH

THE CROWOOD PRESS

First published in 2008 by
The Crowood Press Ltd
Ramsbury, Marlborough
Wiltshire SN8 2HR

www.crowood.com

British Library Cataloguing-in-Publication Data
A catalogue record for this book is available from the British Library.

ISBN 978 1 84797 067 1

Dedication

For Rachael Alia, Christian John and Michael William – my extraordinary children.

Designed and typeset by Focus Publishing, Sevenoaks, Kent

Printed and bound in Malaysia by Times Offset (M) Sdn Bhd

Contents

Fig. 1 Cast lead shot Waterloo figures

Fig. 2 The Airfix 1/12th scale Henry VIII figure.

Introduction

Military figure modelling has existed in one form or another, since man learned both to fight, and to create. Beautifully crafted scale figures of soldiers and sailors have been found in burial sites, pyramids and tombs throughout antiquity, charting and commemorating man's struggle against those who would destroy him, his land and his loved ones. The figures in Fig. 1 are of Wellington, his wife Kitty Pakenham, and an infantry guardsman. They were cast in lead recycled from musket balls retrieved from the field at Waterloo.

Today, we are blessed indeed that a great diversity of model soldiers, sailors and airmen in all scales, from all of the major combatant nations throughout history, are available from some very notable manufacturers across the world. Military figure modelling is no longer the cottage industry it was back in the 1960s and 70s, and the new-found diversity in type and scale can only be a good thing, ensuring in most cases that only the very best have survived.

My own figure-modelling journey began in the early part of the 'swinging sixties'. When I was just a toddler, my parents bought me a beautiful model of Arundel Castle (which, being from 'up north' I thought must be somewhere near Neverland), and a fantastic array of soldiers from across the ages. Britains, Cherilea, Timpo and Benbros were just a small selection from the incredibly rich diversity of then-thriving British manufacturers. The 1960s threw up some very exciting figures from Airfix, including that of Henry VIII in Fig. 2, but nothing could have prepared us for the next decade. In 1970, the year I went to grammar school, I saw *Waterloo* by Dino de Laurentis at the local Odeon. Soon afterwards, as if by magic, the local model shop was stocking the brand-new 54mm 'British Hussar 1815' kit by Airfix in 54mm scale. It was three shillings and sixpence (17.5p), and I couldn't resist it. Thereafter, when pocket money permitted, I bought everything from the Airfix range, but then came the legendary Historex! My best friend at school bought the new Historex catalogue for 1973. In it were startling colour photographs of the most beautiful conversions, all based on the figure range for that year. Ray Lamb not only created the most outstanding figures, but also contributed a chapter on face painting, and shadow and highlight creation. Being a keen artist even then, I applied the guidelines to my artwork; needless to say, my marks at school went up accordingly.

Father's Day 1974 called for a special present. I had seen the range of 54mm figures from Greenwood and Ball in the latest *Military Modelling* magazine, and spotted their range of Sudanese 'Fuzzy Wuzzies', or Beja Ben Amir tribesmen, from the battle at Omdurman. My father had told me that, when he had been in the Army in the Sudan, some of his best friends had been Dervishes, or Fuzzy Wuzzies. I wasn't sure whether to believe him – he had also told me that my grandfather had been shot in the Urals in 1917 – however, there they all were, on the first page of his picture album, wearing the same clothing as the Greenwood and Ball metal

Fig. 3 Greenwood and Ball Dervish 1974 vintage.

figures! I took the painting very seriously and, following guidelines in an article by Roy Dilley, arrived, aged 14, at the result you see in Fig. 3.

Today, 54mm scale (1/32nd) is not as popular as it once was. After Tamiya's entry on to the world modelling stage in the early 1970s, 1/35th scale became a best-seller worldwide.

The figures were designed to accompany and populate the burgeoning number of AFVs in this scale, from makers the world over. Fig. 4 shows some excellent current figure kits – the Tamiya Japanese infantry are still stunning, despite dating originally from the 1970s! There are nowadays a huge proliferation of figure kits

Fig. 4 DML and Tamiya figure kits.

in resin and, for war-gamers (predominantly), polythene. The quality achieved in one-piece polythene mouldings of figures and horses is astounding. The figures in Fig. 5 (Italeri French Artillery) are included in a project later in this volume; for the novice figure modeller and painter, they make an ideal, no-fuss introduction to figure modelling in 1/32nd scale, especially when mated to components from the re-issued Multipose kits from Airfix (Fig. 6). Their price is also appealing, as a comparable model cast in white metal can cost up to 100 times more!

Finally, Fig. 7 shows what can be done with

Fig. 5 Italeri Napoleonic gun team.

Fig. 6 Airfix Multipose re-issues.

1/16th scale figures from the likes of Dragon, Trumpeter and Tamiya. The figure to the left of the picture is their 'German Heavy Machine Gunner' in a greatcoat, converted to a photographer from one of the Nazi propaganda units based in Russia in 1942. With a camera based on one from my own collection, he makes an interesting alternative to a figure 'straight from the box'. Whatever figures are modelled by the major manufacturers, there will always be a little 'wiggle room' for those starting out in the hobby, and looking for something that little bit different – an arm here, a leg there – and using a little imagination can make all the difference when you need to create something original.

Fig. 7 Excellence in 1/18th scale from Tamiya.

CHAPTER 1

Tools for the Job

The tools required for military figure conversions can be as numerous, or as few, as you desire. Your model-making challenges may eventually require the use of a post-drill or a watch-maker's lathe, but in most cases, to get you started in the hobby, all you will need is a sharp craft knife or scalpel, with replaceable blades, along with some differently graded sheets of fine emery paper, paint, brushes and glue. This is not an expensive hobby, nor does it need to be made so by the purchase of masses of extraneous material (at least to start with).

REFERENCE MATERIAL

You will need reference material for uniforms, and for the stance and proportions of particular humans and animals if you want to get the very best results from model-making, but you do not need to pay a fortune for books if you shop around. The Crowood Press has a wide-ranging list of military titles. Second-hand bookshops usually have an excellent military history section, and the public libraries are free. Monthly periodicals such as the legendary *Military Modelling* magazine, and the newer, but no less exciting *Scale Military Modelling International* carry a wealth of information on building, painting and finishing of military figures and armour/softskin subjects. The most important thing to remember is that this hobby should be fun. When the world is a little too much to bear, when relationships are just a little too hard, there is always an escape – go modelling! The hobby should come with its

own slogan: 'Free with every model – *you*!' If you are an experienced modeller there should be something for you in this book. If you are new to the hobby, don't worry. It's easier than it looks sometimes, and if you are not entirely happy with your results, you can make the definitive model next time. Everyone has to start somewhere.

CUTTING

Fig. 8 shows some of the 'cutting-edge' products necessary for accurate trimming, slicing and paring of plastic and resin figure components. Choose tools that feel right in your hand. If you need to apply a lot of pressure in order to sever an arm or leg, use a large blade in a large holder; thinner items may snap and injure you, or others. Back in the 1970s, a friend of mine lost the snapped-off end of his scalpel blade. Unbeknownst to him, the offending 8mm or so of blade tip had 'pinged' off into the long fur coat of his wire-haired fox terrier. When the dog went off for his monthly short back and sides, both he and the groomer got a shock, quite literally, as the blade became lodged in the electric clippers! If you do use a knife with disposable blades, always dispose of the blades responsibly.

Other cutting, particularly of thicker body parts such as waists, should be done carefully with a jigsaw. The saw-type shown in Fig. 9 is available from a range of outlets, from a good model shop to the 'pound shops' on the high street – remember that in most cases you will

Fig. 8 Develop the practised hand of a surgeon.

get exactly what you pay for. The snips and scissors shown in Figs. 10 and 11 are extremely useful when removing components from their sprues or runners. They can be used for basic 'surgery', where an elbow or knee joint needs to be severed, and the resultant damage to components does not present a problem to the build. The circle cutter in Fig. 11 is great for cutting out templates, circles of copper/brass, and semi-circular components to make up uniform items from plastic sheet and card or paper (*see* chapters on John Lynn VC, and the Dancing Cossacks). The drill in Fig. 12 is a small, transformer-based item that can be used for hollowing out and drilling of smaller components. With the use of burr attachments, it can be used to hollow out solid helmets, or add crease/seam detail to an arm, leg or torso. Test as many examples as you can before you buy any powered tool, and try to choose the item that is most controllable speed-wise, and is as vibration-free and adaptable as possible.

HOLDING

Fig. 13 shows an excellent tool for securely holding down a model figure, and identifying detail that might otherwise elude you. If you do

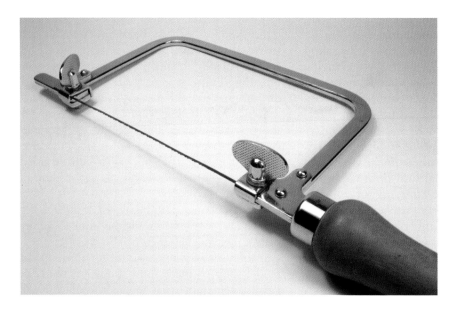

Fig. 9 Jigsaw for more advanced surgery.

Fig. 10 Cut cleanly with the sharpest implements.

Fig. 11 Circle cutters should be used in stages to prevent their warping.

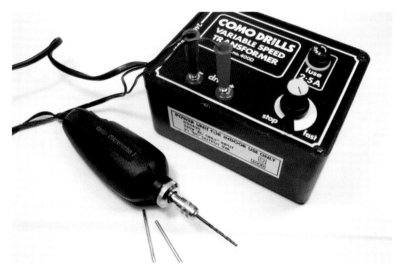

Fig. 12 Drill slowly, and always choose 'HSS' bits.

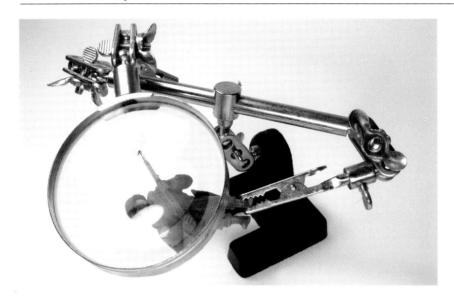

Fig. 13 Clamping devices aid precision and save your eyes.

not possess one of these items, hand-holding of your model and paintbrush is made much easier if the heel of each hand is supported by a worktop throughout the process. Alternatively, simply pin the chap (or chappess) to the modelling surface with one hand, carefully applying the paint or small component with the other. If you do decide to acquire one of these clamps, you may be surprised to discover just how cost-effective they are. Any item that aids the addition of more and finer detail has to be a good thing. Practice for all modellers is equally necessary, but left-handers do find some of the tools and techniques of the 'right-handed world' difficult to master. Fortunately, 'lefties' can now buy a whole range of suitable, purpose-built tools at very reasonable prices – check online and in the trade press for details.

Fig. 14 shows more aids to better vision. You may be able to see detail perfectly well through a lupe like the Fuji one shown here, but if you feel that you also need glasses, even the off-the-shelf numbers shown here, always consult an optician – your eyes are one model-making tool that you cannot replace.

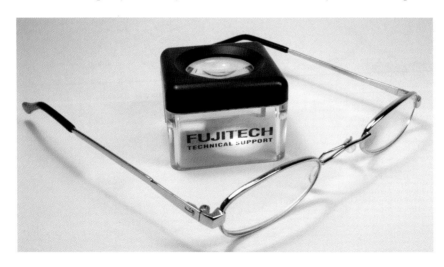

Fig. 14 Care for your eyes. Glasses will also protect from drilled shards.

GLUEING AND FILLING

The miniature clamp shown in Fig. 15 is a very useful little item, which can keep your model components securely in place whilst model-glue (Fig. 16), is curing. There are now strict EU rules governing the manufacture of modern adhesives, and you will find that model-glue for polystyrene plastics is very safe (as long as you do not try gargling with it!). However, if you decide to use 'super-glue', or cyanoacrylate adhesive, a good deal of care needs to be taken. Always ventilate your work area well, by opening a window or switching on an extractor fan, and wear a face mask, either a paper one or a charcoal-based type. If you use an activator, the super-glue will set almost immediately. The chemical content of this agent is immediately apparent if you do get a whiff of it. The activator is a catalyst which produces an exothermic reaction, giving off extreme heat whilst curing the glue in a matter of seconds. These chemicals have obvious advantages, but

Fig. 15 Miniature cramping device, useful in diorama construction.

great care must always be taken in their use. Model fillers are now plentiful and available in a variety of grades, from smooth to coarse (Fig. 17). Do not be afraid to experiment with these, but take care to build them up in layers – a great lump of the material can take for ever to dry.

Fig. 16 Adhesive use requires care at all times.

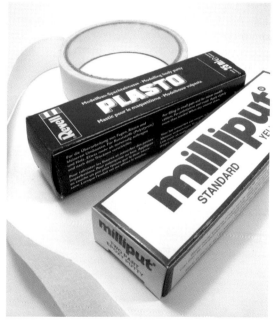

Fig. 17 Model fillers now comply with EU safety rules.

Fig. 18 Sable brushes should be your weapon of choice where possible.

PAINTING AND FINISHING

Paint and its application is a highly personal and subjective affair. A technique that suits one modeller will not necessarily suit another. The ranges of enamel and acrylic paints currently available to model-makers are quite adequate to achieve perfectly acceptable, and often stunning, finishes. The more adventurous will experiment with artist's oil and tempera colours, which in the right hands can produce incredible rendering of skin and cloth textures.

The brushes in Fig. 18 are of a very high quality indeed. This is one area in which attempting to economize is not appropriate. You will need a range of different-sized brushes, from 000 for eyes, to sizes 6–8 for covering larger areas of cloth and kit (depending on the scale in which you decide to work). Buy sable brushes wherever possible and be fastidious, yet gentle, in the cleaning of them. I still use two sable brushes that I have had since the mid-1970s – and not because I'm a bit tight! The point of a well-kept No.2 brush will deliver a dot of paint as small as that of a No.00, as long as it has been well tended with the relevant thinners and water. Fig. 19 shows the Iwata

Fig. 19 Iwata airbrushes give excellent results and are low-maintenance.

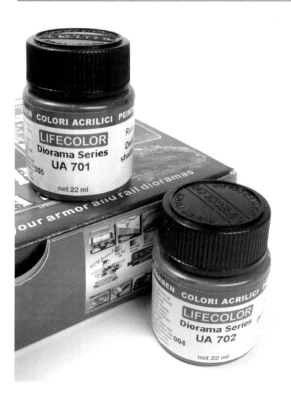

Fig. 20 Airbrush colours are often pre-thinned.

Fig. 21 Staple acrylic colours have tremendous covering power.

airbrush that has become my 'weapon of choice' lately. The Cuirassier chapter (*see* page 58) shows a conventional brush-painted finish with some airbrushed detail, whilst the Boer War chap's finish (see page 80) is more heavily airbrushed. Both methods have their merits, and will achieve the best overall results for you when working together in harmony.

Figs. 20 to 23 illustrate a tiny cross-section of the paint varieties now available to modellers worldwide. Always take care to use and keep these items responsibly, especially if you have small children in the house. Different paint types have different characteristics. Acrylics tend to dry rapidly (unless mixed with water, or another 'wetting' agent), but do cover extraordinarily well. Enamels are the 'old friend' of the modeller, and have recently undergone a change of recipe in order to drag them into the twenty-first century, making

them much more easy to handle than they were in the 1970s. Aerosols are great if you need to cover a good deal of surface area very quickly, but care is needed to build up fine layers gradually. A thick coat will sag, and leave an unevenly coated surface. Pigments such as those from the outstanding MIG range (Fig. 24) are a great way to add surface coverings of

Fig. 22 Old faithful enamels are still popular.

Fig. 24 MIG powder pigments have a multiplicity of applications.

Fig. 23 Cover large areas quickly.

dust to a Desert War figure, or mud to the boots of a Dragoon who has just returned from Waterloo. As with all 'extras', make sure to look carefully at the detail requirements of the model's environment and do not be afraid to experiment.

Diorama accessories are plentiful now. The snow used in the Cossack project (*see* page 138) is illustrated in Fig. 25. It is one of a vast range of items available, primarily aimed at railway modellers, which are equally applicable to military modelling. Trees can be an area of contention, scale-wise. Instead of scratch-building trees using wire armatures, you may wish to commence by painting, adding to, and adapting commercially available items. Sea grass, available from hobby shops, florists and the like, can make for very realistic trees in all scales. Most importantly, do not be afraid to experiment with items from the 'pot-pourri' of life – a long time ago, modellers used to use real moss!

Fig. 25 Proprietary diorama accessories are now of particularly good quality.

CHAPTER 2

French Napoleonic Artillery

KITS TO USE

Converting model figures is a fascinating pastime, which can become rather costly if you choose models in metal or resin. For those on a budget, who still want to achieve a more than acceptable result, polythene figures (more usually the province of wargamers) set an interesting challenge. In days of yore (the late 1960s to be precise), Airfix in the UK marketed an excellent range of 54mm (1/32nd scale) figures, which latterly included French and British Napoleonic troops alongside the more readily available German Stormtroopers (*see*

Fig. 26) and British Commandos. In the early 1970s I set about converting some of them, using the polythene figure as a basis, adding components from the Airfix 54mm range moulded in the more usual styrene. There were mixed results! The major problem was the method of fixing the two plastic types. I tried conventional model-glue, contact-adhesive, and melting/pinning with a match, before bowing to the inevitable disappointment. Needless to say, times have changed. Along with the new century came super-glue, and its activator (a spray catalyst that sets the applied glue in seconds). The hover-boards and silver

Fig. 26 1970s Airfix polythene German infantry figures.

suits of my imagination may not have become reality, but at least there is now a sure way to fix a roughened polythene surface to a polystyrene one!

Italeri have now begun to produce a very good range of polythene figures in 1/32nd scale, including figures, horsemen and artillery from throughout the ages, moulded in a slightly harder plastic than their predecessors in the 1970s. They do need a good wash with detergent to rid them of their coating of mould-release agent. I chose the French Napoleonic line artillery teams, along with a box of Mamelukes, and as you can see in Figs. 27 and 28, I was not disappointed. For the price, these figures are unbeatable – at this scale, a white-metal cast equivalent could cost up to 100 times as much! There are compromises, but many of

these can be rectified with careful use of the still-excellent Airfix Multipose figures (Fig. 29), as you will see.

THE HISTORY

This diorama depicts the artillery team crossing a small wooden bridge, during the French Imperial Army's advance into the Russian homeland. Their advance is checked, as the bridge, which has been weakened by the retreating Russians, begins to collapse. The Mamelukes guarding them have spotted movement in the nearby woods...

When Napoleon returned from his ravages in Egypt, he brought with him much hard-earned experience, and a company of 300 or so Mamelukes. These men, of Circassian,

Fig. 27 Italeri French Imperial Line Artillery in polythene.

*Fig. 28 Italeri
Mameluke cavalry are
very cost-effective.*

Georgian and Armenian descent, were deserters from the armies of Ibrahim Pasha and Murad Bey. They were by far the most flamboyant and fierce troops of any army of the time, and are seen in the diorama protecting the artillery train.

CREATING THE MODEL

Figure One

This is quite an easy conversion as long as you bear in mind the cardinal rule of polythene: never sand it, unless you intend to glue it, preferably at a joint! In Figs. 30 and 31 the figures from the limber are seen in their conjoined state. Their faces are dreadful by comparison with the rest of the figures in the range (for example, the Mamelukes), and the eyes suggest some sort of genetic abnormality. Before removing the head, the selected figure, who is to remain seated, must be surgically removed from his close friend (Fig. 32). Select a very fine-toothed blade for your jigsaw, and strike an imaginary median between the arms and legs (elbows and knees), as in Fig. 32. Saw through slowly, checking the progress from front and rear throughout the process. Always push the blade slightly toward the figure

Fig. 29 Airfix Multipose limb and head donors.

to be discarded (*see* Fig. 33). As a result, the figure selected will usually retain a little of the arm of the other. This gives you a little extra plastic to carve, but will ensure that you end up with a 'complete' arm that can be carved more effectively, with creases being rendered more realistically. Remember that there is no effective way to emery the figure, so your carving skills must be absolute – they will develop with practice, and these figures provide a cost-effective medium on which to carry out that practice. Fig. 34 shows the carving completed, while Fig. 35 shows the newly formed creases, teased out carefully with the tip of a scalpel blade.

Fig. 36 shows the new head in place (in this

21

case from the Airfix Multipose British Infantry set). Slice the busby from the head of the figure first, as this gives you more to hold on to when you come to cut off the head. Place the figure on its back against the cutting mat. Then cut downwards with a stout knife blade, removing the hat in one go if possible. This done, repeat the process for the head at the neck/collar-top juncture. After trimming the mould-lines and cranium top from the Airfix head, lightly sand the figure's neck stub and put in place a tiny blob of cyanoacrylate adhesive (after checking that the room is adequately ventilated)

between the neck and the neck base of the new head. Once it has set, repeat the process with the busby, and spray the whole area with a tiny amount of activator. This will dry very quickly, following an exothermic, chemical reaction between it and the super-glue – fingers and nostrils should be protected at all times! Fig. 37 illustrates the point at which you should trim and fill the neck joint. Once complete, trim all of the mould-lines from around the polythene, remembering to make clean, light cuts with a new blade, as no sanding or scraping is allowed.

Fig. 30 Surgery required at hip and arm junctures.

Fig. 31 Poorly sculpted facial features require attention.

Fig. 32 The cutting point must be assessed from all angles.

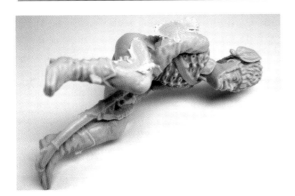

Fig. 33 Remove excess plastic carefully with a scalpel.

Fig. 34 Trimming now complete.

Fig. 35 Carefully carve out crease detail.

Fig. 36 New Airfix Multipose head fitted.

Fig. 37 Trim excess from base of neck.

Figure Two

This chap has felt the bridge giving way and, having left the limber, is going back to help his friend. Figs. 38, 39 and 40 show the figure (from the French Artillery set that only contains guns and crews), who usually lights the fuse atop the cannon. It is important to assess him from every angle to assure yourself of his suitability for the relevant conversion. As he is to be reaching out to his compatriot, this stance is perfect for the purposes of this model.

Figs. 41 and 42 show the head's removal (as on Figure One), and subsequent trimming. Fig. 43 shows the Airfix head glued in place. The busby (Fig. 44) is removed from the original head, level with the hat's base. Fig. 45 reveals the busby and new Multipose hand in place. Remember that the hand positions can be changed easily by a rotation of the wrist before fixing takes place. If you have not already done it, now is a good time to remove the mould-lines and excess 'flash'.

Fig. 38 Front right of figure with ignition taper.

Fig. 39 Rear left of figure before surgery commences.

Fig. 40 Remove mould lines with sharp blade.

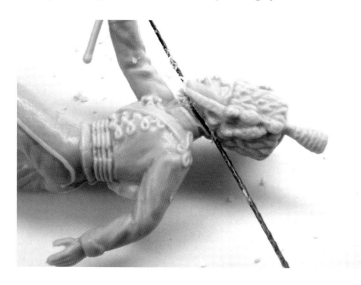

Fig. 41 Remove the head with a fine jigsaw blade.

24

Fig. 42 Trim away the excess polythene.

Fig. 43 Airfix head fixed in place with super-glue.

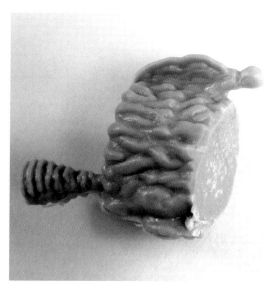

ABOVE: *Fig. 44 Underside of busby detail before trimming.*

RIGHT: *Fig. 45 New hand in place from Multipose kit.*

Figure Three

This figure is reacting to the noise behind, and is looking over his shoulder in order to observe the reaction of the adjacent horse. The conversion takes the same course as the previous ones (Figs. 46 to 49), except that the right arm is replaced with an Airfix item, as shown in Fig. 50. This picture illustrates the necessity to cut the top of this arm short from the shoulder, in order to fit below the level of the bottom of the epaulette. Some testing of the fit will need to be done before the glue is applied. Try to cut the arm's top portion at an angle, so that its joint underneath the epaulette will be hidden once it is glued in place. Figs. 51 and 52 show the best 'assessment' views. Any excess super-glue/activator residue (as seen in Fig. 53) should be carefully removed, once the assembly has thoroughly dried.

Fig. 46 Front view of kit figure before surgery.

Fig. 47 Rear of selected figure showing detail definition.

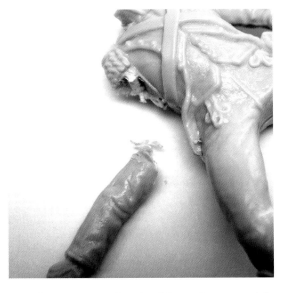

Fig. 48 Arm severed at shoulder – clean cut with heavy blade.

ABOVE: *Fig. 49 Assess the best position for, and choice of, arm.*

RIGHT: *Fig. 50 New Airfix arm being tested.*

Fig. 51 Front right view with arm in place.

Fig. 52 Completed joint viewed from the rear.

The Horse

You may wish to convert more of the horses, but this one is closest to the noise of the collapsing bridge at this time, and is reacting to the sudden change in load distribution. A horse at this juncture would want to 'buck' the traces. In so doing, his first reaction would be to throw his head back, and paw at the ground. Fig. 53 illustrates the difference between the heavy artillery horse and the galloping 'donor' horse from the Mameluke set. In Fig. 54, it is clear that the front, right leg has been removed from the horse, with judicious use of the jigsaw. The angle selected was 62 degrees to the horizontal when seen from the front. This should be marked with an indelible marker before very closely observed cutting commences. The corresponding leg from the Mameluke horse should be removed after being cut at the same angle, but so that the leg turns slightly outward, as the horse tries to redistribute its weight according to instinct.

Sever the donor horse's head in the time-honoured way (see Fig. 55). Fig. 56 shows the new head in place. Remember that the horse's bridle straps, and its lack of 'blinkers' over the eyes, will need to be rectified using plastic sheet and strip, so that they correspond with the other horses' accoutrements. Fig. 57 shows the leg super-glued into place, after the opposing

Fig. 53 The Artillery nag and its Mameluke donor horse.

Fig. 54 Cut new right foreleg from Mameluke horse.

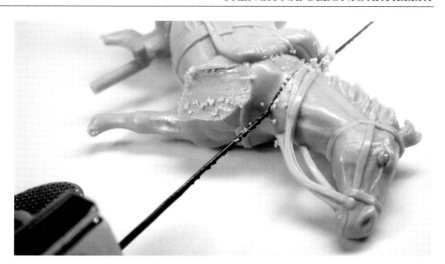

Fig. 55 Remove horse heads with care.

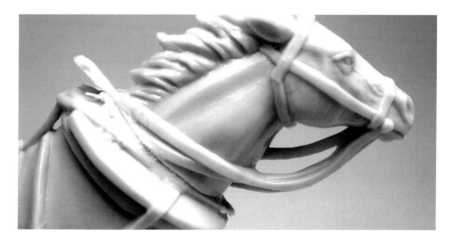

Fig. 56 New Mameluke horse head in place.

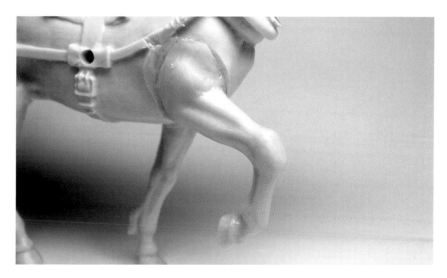

Fig. 57 New foreleg fixed using super-glue.

Fig. 58 Check stance from all angles.

faces to be affixed have been roughened to a keying surface, with coarse emery paper. Fig. 58 illustrates well the final stance of the animal, before you commit to the filling and sanding stage. Check the leg joint closely (Fig. 59), and assess the need for sparing use of model filler.

Fig. 60 shows the need for filler and a little sanding. It may be better, in some cases, to fill the gap with glue and activator, so as to preserve the strength of the joint, which may otherwise be compromised by the vibrations associated with excessive sanding.

Fig. 59 Foreleg inner joint and muscle detail.

Fig. 60 Fill joint with super-glue and activator mix.

The Gun

The artillery pieces included in this diorama are from the Gribeauval system of artillery adopted by the French First Empire. The major problem comes in the form of holes (to take the cleats), and gaps in which the extra barrel spigots (for longer barrels) sit. These are all on the tops of the carriage sides (*see* Fig. 61). Fill the relevant areas with model filler and, once it has set, cut two 3 3 12mm strips from 20-thou plastic strip. Using super-glue, affix these to the rail tops as in Fig. 62. The finished article is shown in Fig. 63.

Fig. 61 Take care to fill all unnecessary holes and joints.

Fig. 62 Fix new iron banding strips in place using plastic strip.

Fig. 63 Finished assembly with detailing complete.

The Mamelukes

Fig. 64 illustrates the folly of a middle-aged, yet still optimistic modeller. This is what happens, nine times out of ten, if polythene figures are not washed with a degreasant before paint is applied. Figs. 65 and 66 illustrate the degreasing process. A strong washing-up liquid will suffice, but an equally strong scrubbing brush will also be required to remove the mould-release agent still coating the entire surface of the model. Figs. 67 and 68 show the excellent, smooth finish that can be achieved with only two coats of acrylic paint from a simple aerosol can. In Fig. 69 the Mamelukes are seen in action.

This is an immensely enjoyable project, requiring a minimum of effort and producing an impressive and very cost-effective result. The entire project can be completed for the price of a 1/35th scale Tiger Tank kit, so hats off to both Italeri and Airfix!

Fig. 64 Precisely what not to do with your horse!

Fig. 65 Scrub with a soft-bristled brush.

Fig. 66 Use a degreasant in all of the creases.

Fig. 67 An excellent finish using a proprietary aerosol.

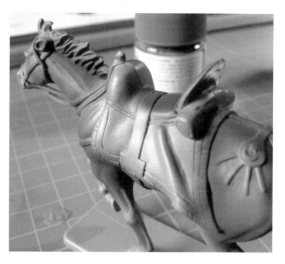

Fig. 68 Shadows applied using an airbrush.

Fig. 69 Mamelukes at the gallop in full dress uniform.

ARTILLERY AND DIORAMA FURTHER REFERENCE

Fig. 70 Master gunner of the Imperial Artillery train.

Fig. 71 Wheel horse and rider in campaign garb.

ABOVE: *Fig. 72 Bridge over the Don river collapses.*

LEFT: *Fig. 73 Rear view of artillery train.*

ABOVE: *Fig. 74 Troops reacting to distant cannonade.*

Fig. 76 Uncoupling the horses at speed may save the gun team.

BELOW: *Fig. 75 Mamelukes on anti-partisan duty.*

ABOVE: *Fig. 77
Front right view.
Note finished horse
stance revisions.*

LEFT: *Fig. 78
Artillery train on
the Russian border
1812.*

CHAPTER 3

Cuirassier, 1815

THE HISTORY

The French Heavy Battle Cavalry, which Napoleon created in the early 1800s, became known as the Cuirassiers. The name was derived from their wearing of the distinctive breast and back armour known as the 'cuirass', an item used in a cruder form by Spanish Conquistadors several centuries earlier. Cuirassiers were amongst the most fierce and able troops in the Grande Armée, thundering to glory on the heaviest horses available, in their capacity as the 'weapon of mass decision'. By the eve of the Battle of Waterloo, they had played a critical role in each of Bonaparte's battles, from Maida to Waterloo.

The 1/16th scale kit of the French Cuirassier from Mini Art in the Ukraine will form the basis for this conversion. The kit is an excellent representation of the subject, but you will find a few slightly difficult areas. There are one or two corrections to be made, but these are, in fact, very few, and do not detract from the overall excellence of the figure and horse, whether converted or not.

CREATING THE MODEL

The Horse
The finished figure of the Cuirassier's mount is truly exquisite. My example, however, needed some dutiful clamping and filling. The hair on the horse's flanks is very well replicated, so it is wise to go carefully at the sanding stage. Figs. 79, 80 and 81 show jointing in various

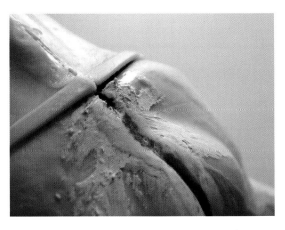

Fig. 79 Breast jointing aided with super-glue.

Fig. 80 The belly strap needs careful alignment before glueing.

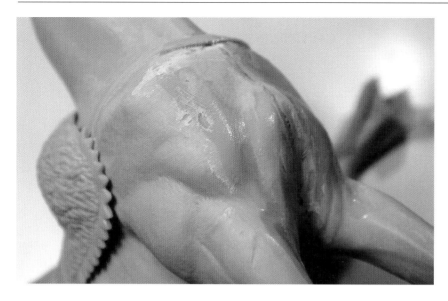

Fig. 81 Joints now glued and filled.

positions along the longitudinal, central-meeting position of the two horse halves. Glue the left and right halves with cyanoacrylate adhesive where the portions actually touch one another. To make life a little easier, use a thick consistency of the super-glue along with a little activator (as always, in a well-ventilated space). You will find that the glue cures almost immediately, so be careful not to include your fingers in the finished model. There will be gaps, most likely at each end, so fill them as

shown in Fig. 79 with a quick-setting modelling putty.

When dry, the assembly should be sanded lightly along the joint until the gap disappears, taking care to retain the accurate replication of the muscle shape. In Fig. 82 the strap around the base of the horse's tail is protected from the model filler, which is trimmed away carefully with a scalpel, or similar. Sand around this area carefully in order to preserve the skin texture on the rear quarters. If you are in any doubt about

Fig. 82 Tail strap should be added when joints are fixed and filled.

Fig. 83 Bedding roll in place with incision, and curvature induced.

Fig. 84 New straps added from plastic strip.

the integrity of the tail/body joint, use superglue as this is a 'delicate' area of the horse once the model is complete.

In Fig. 83, the bedding roll on the rear of the saddle is dissected. Unfortunately the kit-supplied item is very straight and rigid, lacking the radius needed to 'sit' properly atop the saddle's rear. Use a fine-bladed jigsaw to perform this particular surgery, before mounting on the saddle. Fill the resultant gap with model filler once the two halves are glued

in place. Fig. 84 shows the rolled saddle blanket in place with new straps fitted, from 10-thou strip. The new straps should butt up to the strap ends of the moulded-on straps and be cut to shape, so surrounding the two rolls. Fig. 85 shows the process completed before the ends are trimmed. Finally, sand the whole assembly with extremely fine emery paper to dispel any large plastic burrs. The sheepskin fleece saddle blanket and saddle are then assembled and fitted as per the supplied kit instructions.

Fig. 85 Straps fastened into place on bed roll.

The Cuirassier

Assembling the body of the rider presents a few problems with regards to the fit of the body-part halves. The right leg shown in Fig. 86 glues together nicely once it is held as shown, with masking tape. There is, however, quite a pronounced 'trough' at each side of the joint – perhaps an aberration from the moulding process. Once the glue has set, both leg components must be filled where necessary along their respective joint lines. Fig. 87 shows the moulding 'trough'. Fig. 88 illustrates the delicate sanding needed in order to preserve the integrity of the component.

The cuirass portion of the upper torso is shown assembled in Fig. 89. The two body halves fit together well and require careful alignment before sanding of the resultant joint takes place. The torso is shown completed in Fig. 90, having been sanded at the main joints. Joints such as those at the front and back faces of the trouser legs should be fine-sanded before

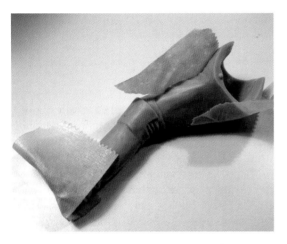

Fig. 86 Trooper's leg joint aided by masking tape.

Fig. 87 Moulding imperfections are apparent in some joints.

Fig. 88 Delicately sand all joints with fine emery paper.

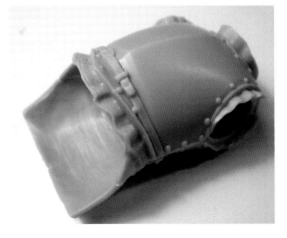

Fig. 89 Torso jointing details and correct alignment.

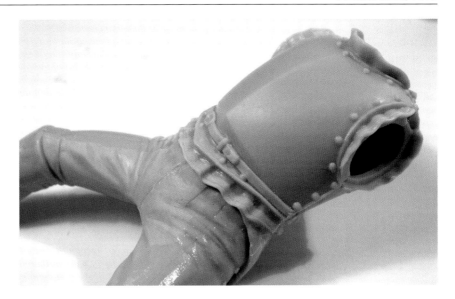

Fig. 90 Joining of torso and leg assemblies.

a thin coating of model-glue is run along the joined portion. This very slightly melts the plastic in order to produce a smoother seam – be careful not to overdo it, and at the same time remember to keep your fingers clean and glue-free. Fig. 91 shows the saddle and fleece cover detail. This portion of the build should be completed by this stage in order that the legs can be checked for fit, as they will occupy this position when the model is complete. Any problems with the legs not fitting snugly to the

saddle can be rectified by gently trimming the crotch with a scalpel – not for the faint-hearted!

Next, for the head and collar, the two rear halves must be severed (*see* Fig. 94). The two resultant collar halves should then be cemented in place on the shoulders (Fig. 93) and the remaining three portions of the head (two backs and a face) assembled separately (*see* Fig. 95). Join the head parts very carefully in order to obviate as much as possible the need for any filling of the resultant joints. In order to

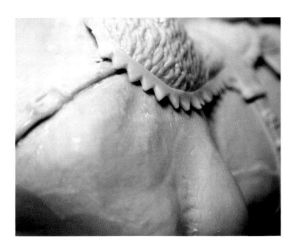

Fig. 91 Saddle and saddle blanket detail.

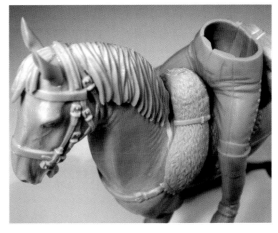

Fig. 92 Test-fit legs to assess correct upright posture of figure.

Fig. 93 Collar requires careful edge trimming for a perfect fit.

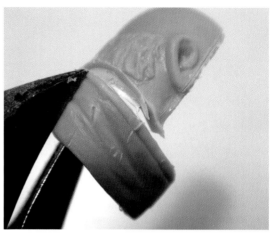

Fig. 94 Remove collar from base of neck.

re-install the head in the attitude required – turned to the right of centre (accepting the Emperor's salute) – glue it to the top of the collar (*see* Fig. 96). Fig. 97 shows the resultant gap left from the surgery, which should be filled and carefully sanded (*see* Fig. 98). Whilst glueing the head in the required attitude, make sure that you examine the assembly from every angle in order to achieve a realistic positioning. Have a look at people around you to double-check their neck posture and attitude.

Helmet
Fig. 99 deals with the assembly of the two halves of the Dragoon-style helmet. The halves require careful alignment, but are a very good fit, requiring a little trimming, but no filling. Fig. 100 shows an old-fashioned approach to soldier modelling that I picked up from the venerable Historex catalogue during the 1970s. Take a new scalpel blade and, having secured the kit-plume to a flat surface, slice downwards in a random pattern around the circumference,

Fig. 95 Assemble head, taking great care with alignment.

Fig. 96 Replace head in revised position after trimming and sanding.

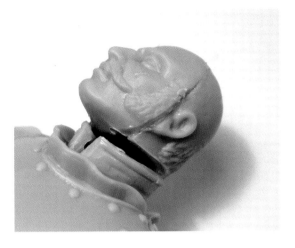

Fig. 97 Resultant jointing gap before filling.

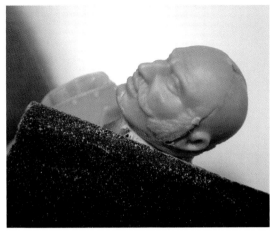

Fig. 98 Careful sanding will pay dividends at the painting stage.

and down the length of the plume. This teases out the individual moulded-in feathers to form a more realistic plume. Once it is complete, coat with model-glue, deep into the root of each liberated feather, and leave to dry for 24 hours in order to preserve the finished item's integrity and strength (*see* Fig. 101).

The next step is to add the chin-strap (Fig. 102). Be careful to leave a substantial gap in between the ends of the two components, in order that the helmet will fit on and off the cuirassier's head. This will enable you to test-fit during construction, and leave the helmet as a separate component during the painting procedure.

Arms
Few modellers have made a really detailed study of anatomy, but your own body, or that of a friend, is an excellent place to start your observations. If you look down at your right arm, and alternately inwards, keeping your

Fig. 99 Helmet halves align readily and require little trimming.

Fig. 100 Plume feather detail added with new scalpel blade.

Fig. 101 Plume in place on helmet side.

upper arm stiff, you will find that your right forearm swivels easily to the right. This should be emulated when you are modifying the right (sabre) arm from the kit, to hold the staff of the standard in the correct attitude. Fig. 103 shows the exact position of the necessary cut, and how it is made with a fine jigsaw blade, once the arm is assembled and secured to a flat surface. In Figs. 104 and 105 the re-glued arm is shown from both sides before the filler is applied to the resultant gap. Fig. 106 shows the filler applied and carefully sanded to replicate the trough of the sleeve's crease. Sand using a very fine emery in order to preserve and emulate the texture of the surrounding plastic. Figs. 107 and 108 show how to coat the joints with glue and trim the edges of the old folds before re-sanding to the new shape revealed in Fig. 109.

Hands

The hands supplied with the kit both need a little trimming to achieve the required attitude. The right hand (Fig. 110) comes with the sword hilt, pommel and straps moulded integrally with the gloved hand. After delicate and judicious use of a fine scalpel blade the hand should resemble more the one shown in Fig. 111. As is usual during this type of procedure, the hand must be gripped tightly (perhaps in a miniature vice), and the sharpest

Fig. 102 Chin-strap glued carefully in place. This will part readily when put in place on head.

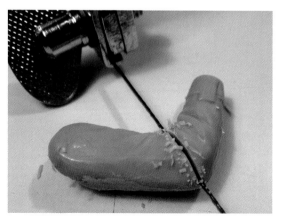

Fig. 103 Elbow joint surgery under way.

Fig. 104 New position of elbow joint.

Fig. 105 Resultant gap before filling occurs.

Fig. 106 Filler applied and sanded smooth.

Fig. 107 Model-glue applied to elbow-joint filler.

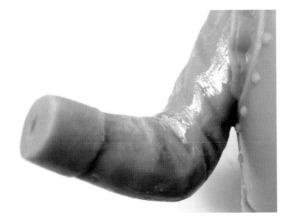

Fig. 108 Creases and uniform folds trimmed and sanded.

Fig. 109 Revised elbow shape from rear.

Fig. 110 Integral hand and hilt assembly.

Fig. 111 Hand after hilt is trimmed away.

Fig. 112 Drill guide-hole with tip of blade.

Fig. 113 Final hole drilled with fine bit.

Fig. 114 Arm assembled in final position.

blade selected. The guide-hole for the major one necessary to hold the staff of the guidon should be started using the fine point of a No.10 or 11 blade or similar in your scalpel or craft knife. Place the tip of the blade at the centre of the area to be drilled and gently rotate until the hole starts to appear (Fig. 112). Fig. 113 shows the hole proper after drilling with a 2mm fine twist drill. Fig. 114 shows the final position of the freshly drilled right hand.

Check the arm in position on the upper torso to ensure the most realistic alignment possible. The left arm (Fig. 115) should be assembled as per the kit instructions, but raised slightly from its projected position in the attitude shown. This will give a realistic appearance to the cuirassier's posture as he controls the horse. A little filling and sanding will be required in order properly to replicate the wrap-around nature of the calfskin gauntlets, and eliminate any jointing gaps.

Fig. 116 shows the correct attitude of the bit and bridle components, which are not clearly shown on the kit's assembly illustrations. Take care when trimming the mould-lines as these parts can easily snap. Fig. 117 illustrates the care needed when jointing the upper torso. Filler will be required in order to ensure that the turn-backs at the bottom of the surcoat are joint-less, and smooth. Be very careful not to compromise the surrounding detail whilst trimming. Always choose a 'path' to sand, which avoids buttons and such.

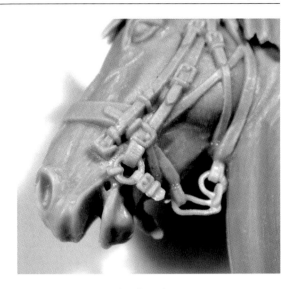

Fig. 116 Bit assembled and in situ.

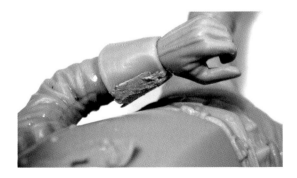

Fig. 115 Gauntlets require sanding to all joints and seams.

Fig. 117 Torso joint glued and sanded.

The Eagle

Figs. 118 to 122 show the eagle and the stages of its construction. This is not as difficult as it may seem, as the critical dimension – the body and head of the eagle – happens to be the same length as a German jackboot in 1/35th scale, which can be 'cannibalized' from any figure in that scale by Dragon, Tamiya, or the like. Take the boot, once removed, and turn it upside down, so that the shoe portion becomes the head of the Eagle. Fig. 119 shows the initial shape to be achieved, by careful, alternating use of the scalpel and emery paper. In Fig. 120 the wings and basic feather details have been added using 20-thou plastic sheet, as per the diagram provided. In Fig. 121, it is beginning to take shape when placed atop the mounting plate and staff top. With the final feather detail added, the eagle is sprayed with a suitable gold finish (Alclad or similar), as shown in Fig. 122.

Fig. 118 Choice of 1/35th scale jackboot for eagle's body.

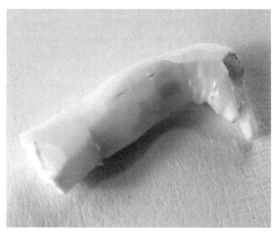

Fig. 119 Shaping of head with scalpel and emery paper.

Fig. 120 Basic eagle shape begins to appear.

Fig. 121 Detail added using plastic strip and rod.

*Fig. 122 Final finish
with paint applied.*

Accoutrements

Stirrup-Cup

The stirrup-cup was originally formed from 6mm thick leather. This version is built up using 5mm diameter plastic tube (Evergreen range, or similar), cut to a length of 4mm. The 2mm wide straps are wrapped around the tube (*see*

Fig. 123). Make sure that the strap-joints are at the side of the assembly that is joined to the stirrup once the assembly is dry. Fig. 124 shows the addition of the braiding to the outer edge-end of each side of the portemanteau. After fixing in the manner shown, take care to radius the outer edge of the braiding with fine emery, to better replicate the cloth braid of the original.

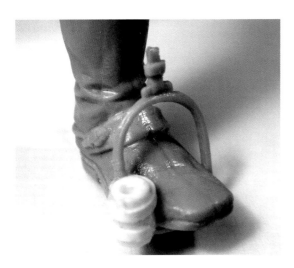

Fig. 123 Stirrup-cup detail from plastic tube and strip parts.

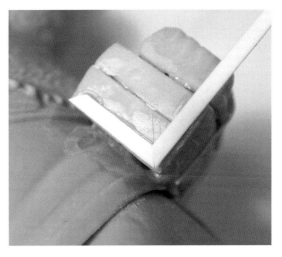

Fig. 124 Valise (portemanteau) detail added with suitable strip.

Fig. 125 New sword-hilt guard and grip details.

The Sword

Fig. 125 illustrates the process of fabricating the hand-grip and forward hilt-guard of the sword, which was removed from around the right hand earlier. It may seem a little odd that a kit manufacturer would want to mould the hand and sword hilt as a one-piece item, but it is often done to keep production costs, and the final cost to the consumer, to a minimum. After the assembly has been left to set for about an hour, the forward hilt-guard, made from 2mm, half-round plastic strip, can be glued in place in the attitude shown in Fig. 126. Trim the excess from the strip and add the other strips as shown in Fig. 127; these form the 'basket' required to protect the hand of the user whilst in combat. Before fixing these components, twist them roughly into shape, securing one end of each strip to the hilt, perhaps with super-glue applied from a cocktail stick. When one end is secured, glue the other ends to the top of the hilt, constantly checking alignment. In Fig. 128 the leather thong and 'tassle' are fitted. The form of the knot is shown on the left side of the photograph, whilst the finished item is shown in-situ on the right. Fig. 129 shows the belt-straps in place, along with the tassle at the end of the thong. These should be integrated at their joint with model filler.

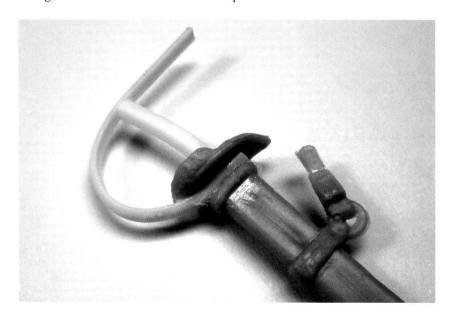

Fig. 126 Secure guard-hilt joint with super-glue.

Fig. 127 Secured basket guard and hilt detail.

Fig. 128 Knotting the hilt adornment in plastic strip.

PAINTING AND FINISHING

General Advice

Although a complete paint job is outside the scope of this chapter, it is possible to give some simple advice that should be useful. This figure and horse were painted in the 'old-fashioned' way, as not everyone is lucky enough to have access to an airbrush, or indeed is keen on using one. Some feel that the results achieved with an airbrush can lack a certain 'ruggedness'. I believe that there is plenty of room for all disciplines and types of finish. Whether you use one type or the other, or a combination, the final result and your appreciation of it should be the deciding factor. Reference to one of the many books on figure painting, or indeed one of the excellent *Military Modelling* magazines, should yield some excellent tips.

Some modellers use enamels, some use acrylics from Tamiya or the excellent Lifecolor range, and the really intrepid ones use artist's oil paints, for the ease and effectiveness of their blending whilst making shadows in clothing creases and facial features. These are incredibly lifelike when completed, but there is a penalty to pay in increased drying times. Years ago, I began my model-painting journey in the company of Humbrol enamels. Their range has recently undergone a review of recipe and their colours are now much more controllable. Fig.

Fig. 129 Addition of scabbard support straps.

130 shows the French Blue base colour, which has been dry-brushed over using a paler shade (mixed Blue/White, 50–50).

Dry-brushing is almost exactly what it sounds like. A No.6 brush is loaded with paint, then wiped on tissue until it is almost dry. Then the brush is flicked to and fro across the promontories of the sleeve creases, leaving a tiny amount of paint residue on the crease tops. The procedure is repeated until the required

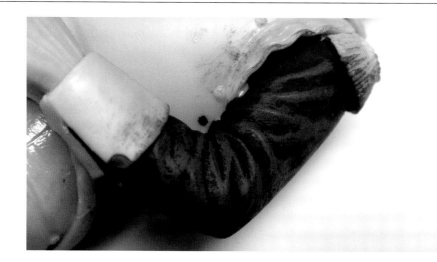

Fig. 130 Dry-brushing of paler blue shade for highlights.

Fig. 131 Silver-plate finish before burnishing.

Fig. 132 Brush marks are eliminated by gentle burnishing.

finish is achieved. A good deal of trial and error will be needed, but it is always important to remember that less is more.

Fig. 131 shows the silver-pigmented paint in place. Alclad and many other companies produce liquid-metal paint finishes that are extremely modeller-friendly. They all come with their own particular set of instructions, but the general advice is to buff and burnish when the paint is dry. In Fig. 132 there are brush marks in evidence on the cuirass. These are removed by localized burnishing with a very soft cloth fragment. The helmet in Fig. 133 is of the Dragoon type (*see also* Fig. 149). The details should be painted using a sable brush if possible. Try to use a No.3 brush, if you can buy sable, as it will hold more paint, minimizing the amount of re-loading you need to do.

When painting the tiniest details, an eyeglass or magnifier can be useful. In order to keep your hands steady, try to brace their outer edges against the table-top. Your fingers will then be steadier and more controllable.

The Standard

The standard, or *guidon*, is manufactured using the accompanying colour diagram. Once you have a colour copy to the correct size (the bottom edge should measure 13.3cm before folding), spray the rear of the paper sheet (160 gsm is best) and wrap the guidon around your previously painted length of plastic rod (3mm diameter). The artwork well represents the hand-wrought quality of the original embroidery, but if you prefer a slightly raised finish to the lettering, this can be achieved by the use of thickish enamel paint of a pale gold colour, carefully applied, using the printed lettering as a guide.

Horse

The horse painting is fairly straightforward if enamels or acrylic paints are used. (I once saw someone paint a horse like this one, but in 54mm scale, using oil paints and sponges! A flat coat was painted on to the horse. Whilst this

Fig. 133 Helmet front detail with plume in place.

was still wet, the painter – the legendary Ray Lamb – dabbed the fine, natural sponges into the horse, and added progressively more pale versions of the base colour, leaving the muscle creases darker. The effect was stunning, and the most lifelike finish of its type that I have ever seen.

The tape 'mask' shown in Fig. 134 is put in place to shield the saddlery during painting. Alternatively, the saddle can be left as a sub-assembly, but it seems to be easier to control and less delicate if it is glued in place on the horse's back in this way. Once the aerosol coat of black has been allowed to dry, the mask is removed (Fig. 135). Fig. 136 shows the basic colours of the saddlery portion of the build, before any shading or highlights are added using the dry-brush technique.

Fig. 137 illustrates the finesse required for successful brush painting. The trick is not to 'fight' with your brushes, and to let them do the work. Practise with the brush on a surface that is similar to that on your model. Try laying the loaded bristles flat on to the surface and 'trace' a line, as you would with your finger. If it is wrong first time, you can always go over it. The fetlock/hoof area benefits from a little dry-brushing to pick up the highlights. The bridle

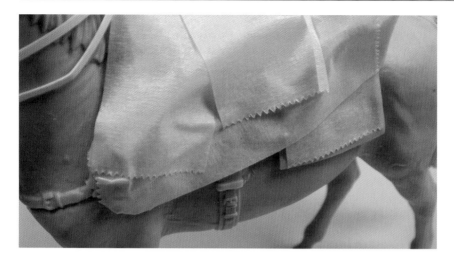

Fig. 134 Mask the saddle area before spraying.

Fig. 135 Remove masking tape carefully once sprayed.

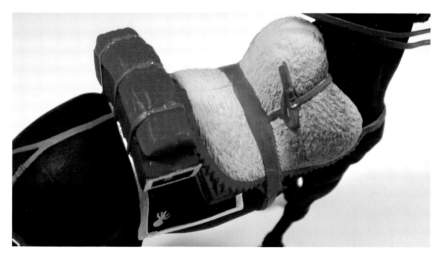

Fig. 136 Separate base colour coats in place.

Fig. 137 Finesse your details with a fine brush.

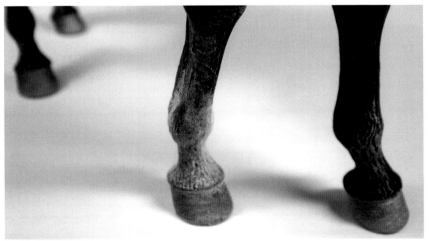

Fig. 138 Dry-brush hooves and fetlock details.

Fig. 139 Appropriate leather tone for new bridle.

detail in Fig. 139 requires very careful brush painting. Always check references before committing to a final colour for the leather work, and remember that it is easier and preferable to darken a colour than to lighten it. Fig. 140 shows how patience and selective, gradually built-up dry-brushing can pay dividends in the rendering of various textures and surfaces.

Figs. 141–143 show the finished item. The flag or *guidon*, a replica of the post-1804 pattern type carried by all Cuirassier regiments until the time of Waterloo, is produced by copying these three illustrations. Copied on to stout paper (120 gsm, or similar), the flag should be folded in half and twisted or bent until the desired shape and 'flutter' is achieved. Before it is cemented in place on the pole, a spray-type glue is used to mate the inner faces of the flag halves. This project is very cheap and satisfying to produce, as long as you take your time and are not afraid to experiment along the way. Time taken at the painting stage will pay great dividends. Figs. 144–147 are vital horse-painting reference shots.

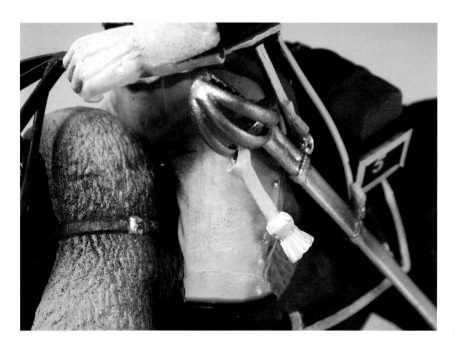

Fig. 140 Selective dry-brushing in action.

Fig. 141 After the battle of Austerlitz.

Fig. 142 Horse hair is painted in gloss black tone.

Fig. 143 Guidon shown in detail on eagle standard.

Fig. 144 Note graduated skin/hair colours and tones.

Fig. 145 Mane details – note points of light on hair and eyeballs.

Fig. 146 Eyelash and ear details.

ABOVE: *Fig. 148 Ewart's eagle in brass captured at Waterloo.*

OPPOSITE: *Fig. 149 5th Cuirassier standard at Waterloo.* (Illustration by the author.)

Fig. 147 Dragoon/Cuirassier headgear. Note plume socket.

CHAPTER 4

Lancashire Fusiliers Mounted Infantry, South Africa, 1900

THE HISTORY

The Lancashire Fusiliers were active throughout the Boer War in their traditional role as elite infantrymen, distinguishing themselves in battle after battle, from Spion Kop to Pretoria. Once peace had been declared, and the resilient Boer army surrendered, the Grens Oorlog, or Bush War, began, wherein the Boer 'bitter-enders', now outlaws in their own land, took to the Bushveld in large numbers to conduct a protracted guerilla war against the occupying British forces. Blockhouses of local stone and the tactically important new material, corrugated iron, or 'crinkly tin' as it became known, were built as bases from which the British Army would conduct patrols on horseback. In the veld, the Boer Kommando was at home. It fell to the British 'Tommy' to adapt, and they did so with relish. The 6th militia battalion of the XX Foot, Lancashire Fusiliers, set off for Port Elisabeth in the Cape, early in 1900. Immediately on their arrival they headed toward Johannesburg, and their new patrol duties. The accompanying period pictures begin the story at Wellington Barracks, Bury. They end in the bush, where the mode and fashion of dress has had to adapt to the extreme conditions of the Highveld.

CREATING THE MODEL

This project is a little more complex than the Cuirassier, but it is easily achievable, and ready to be adapted from various kits currently available at relatively little expense in the model shop. Any of the 1/16th scale Second World War German figures wearing a conventionally cut uniform are suitable for adaptation to British figures of this period. The suit-cut similarities are obvious, and more convincing once the insignia has been removed. I chose to use Dragon's Wehrmacht mounted infantry-man, as the stance is sympathetic to some of those in the Fusilier's reference shots, and the figure is interacting with the horse already.

The Horse

Unfortunately, the horse in the kit is a bit the 'worse for wear' – he will well represent a horse that was raised in South Africa, and has seen his share of campaigning! Figs. 1 to 11 outline the surgery necessary to bring the stance of this horse to something approaching that expected of a military horse in Victorian times (or, indeed, any other times). This is not actually a poor representation straight from the box, but, because of the manner in which my particular example exited the mould, a little remedial work was necessary. If your two body halves do not match precisely, or legs have become splayed or distorted, the following will help. Figs. 150, 151 and 152 amply illustrate the problem if left untreated. Fig. 153 shows a critical part of the filling-in job that needs to be done, in other words, there are large gaps around the ears once they are glued in place. Fig. 154 shows the mid-portion gap that occurs once you attempt to align the body halves longitudinally, the jointing of which requires

RIGHT: *Fig. 150 Rear legs before surgery.*

BELOW: *Fig. 151 Rear fetlocks and accompanying stance problem.*

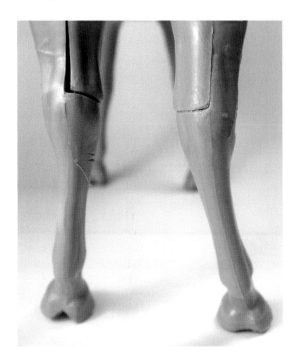

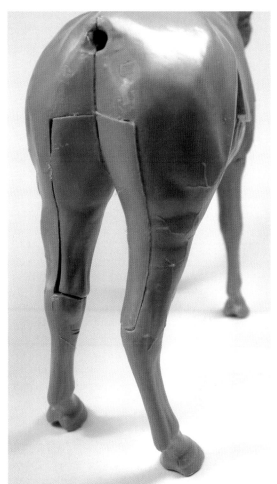

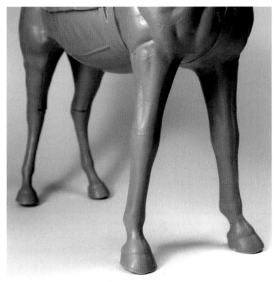

Fig. 152 Front leg stance is too wide.

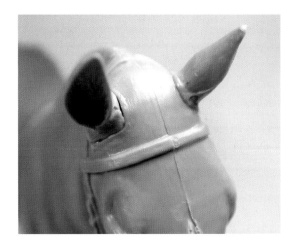

Fig. 153 Ear joints require filling and sanding.

Fig. 154 Stance of horse before surgery commences.

Fig. 155 Surgery commences in upper foreleg portion.

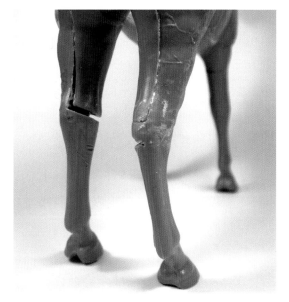

ABOVE: Fig. 156 Cut slot carefully in right leg.

RIGHT: Fig. 157 Alteration detail to right rear leg.

masking tape and clamping around the whole body in order to obtain a strong bond.

In Fig. 155 the surgery begins in earnest. It is important to build the basic horse as far as possible, so that you can assess the extent of remedial work needed as you progress. You should also refer to the reference photographs of real horses included in this chapter, both for stance and, later, colour. Use a jigsaw with a fine-toothed blade to saw the legs in the manner shown, three-quarters of the way through, and from the inside outwards. Fig. 156 illustrates the extent of the rear leg-cutting. First, secure the rear right leg with super-glue and activator, keeping fingers clear, and the surrounding area well ventilated. The horizontal slot sawn on the inner edge of this leg must now be compressed vertically, and joined with super-glue. This will draw the bottom half of the leg inwards, and make the right leg's position much more believable (see Fig. 157). Figs. 158, 159 and 160 show the points at which to fill and, subsequently, sand using fine-grade emery paper. In Figs. 161, 162 and 163, the filling/sanding process has progressed. Spraying the areas with a neutral aerosol colour, once the sanded filler has dried, will reveal any abnormalities and 'lumps' still apparent on the surface of the joints. Sand further until the required, smooth surface is achieved, and the muscle contours have been followed precisely.

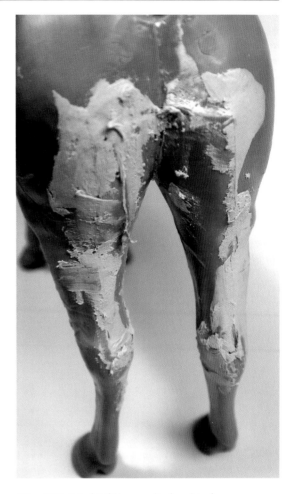

Fig. 158 Model filler applied to hindquarters.

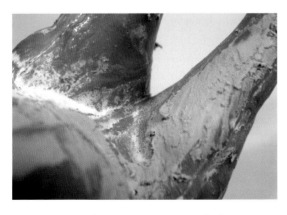

Fig. 159 Rear leg inner portion ready for sanding/trimming.

Fig. 160 Foreleg before trimming commences in earnest.

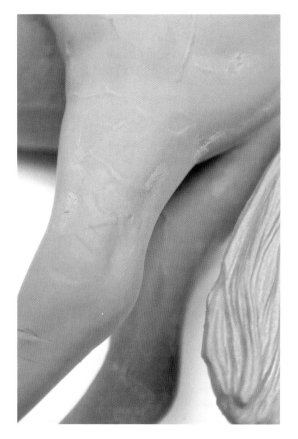

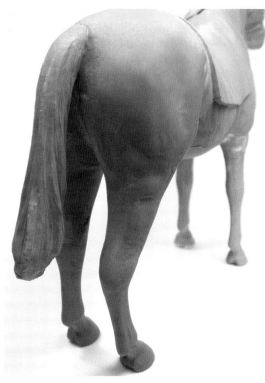

*Fig. 163 Finished rear quarter after sanding/
re-spraying.*

ABOVE: *Fig. 161
Neutral pale buff
spray coat.*

RIGHT: *Fig. 162
Check carefully for
anomalies in the
surface texture.*

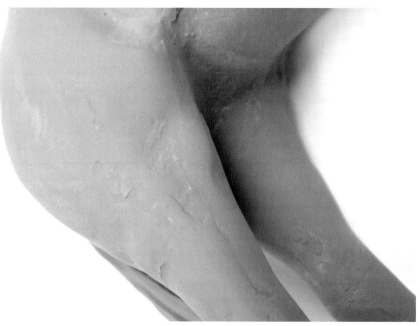

Saddlery

In order to convert the saddle from the German Second World War type to the less well-padded version for the well-dressed Victorian equestrian, you need first to remove the pressure-relieving portions (see Fig. 164). Fig. 165 shows the removal of the straps on the lower portion of the saddle. These are shown cemented together in position atop the moulded-in horse blanket in Fig. 166. This photograph also shows the areas to be removed, just before final sanding takes place. In Fig. 167 the kit's stirrups are assembled. The strap is from 2.5mm wide Evergreen strip, cut to length before passing through the relevant slotted hole. Be sure to hold this joint for about 20 seconds after the glue is applied, in order to ensure a strong bond. Fig. 168 illustrates the saddle top with the necessary portions filled and sanded smooth, better replicating a British Army saddle of this late-Empire period.

The chest-strap is not typical of the period, yet it well illustrates the style of tack worn back home. It is reproduced using 3mm wide portions of plastic strip and joined with a boss from a stretched sprue. Fig. 170 illustrates the belly-band strap with the end retaining loop, made from 3mm strip, in place. Take care to

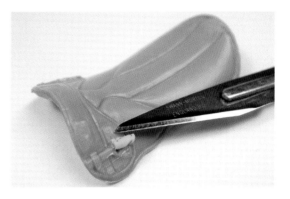

Fig. 164 Saddle-top surgery and trimming of excess detail.

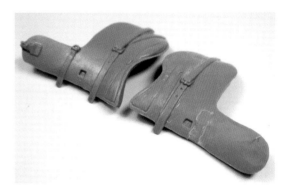

Fig. 165 Saddle sides for comparison.

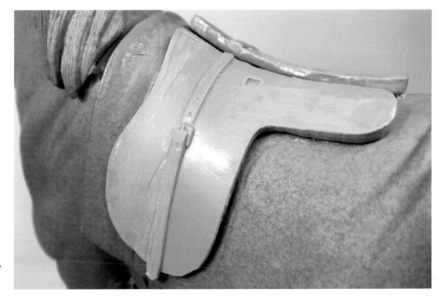

Fig. 166 Lower saddle parts checked in place.

Fig. 167 Stirrup assembly with plastic strip in place.

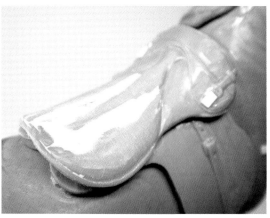

Fig. 168 New saddle-top configuration, Victorian style.

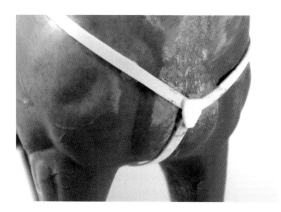

Fig. 169 Revised chest-strap detail now in place.

Fig. 170 Belly band strap retainer from plastic strip.

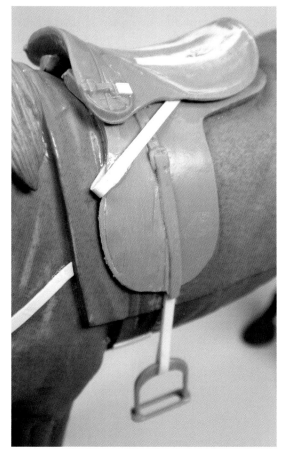

Fig. 171 Straps, stirrups and plastic strip detail.

remove the paint carefully from the strap with a sharp blade, at the point where the loop will fit. If this is not done, the glue will not adhere properly. In Fig. 171 the top saddle portion has been put in place and its retaining straps fitted on both sides. The stirrups and straps are also fitted in the manner shown and any burrs and flash removed with scalpel and fine emery.

Fig. 172 shows the bed roll in its cover, during construction. A 25mm length of 8mm diameter plastic tubing was placed on top of a very warm domestic radiator until the twisting/warping was achieved. In less enlightened times, this would have been achieved using the flame of a candle and some experimentation! Once it has been treated in this way, and once the embryo end-pieces have been put in place, and suitably trimmed, the plastic tube fits neatly across the rear portion of the saddle blanket. Figs. 173 and 174 show the bed roll, and its new 2mm wide 10-thou straps glued in place. The saddle-mounted equipment

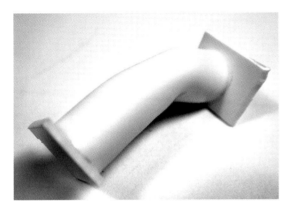

Fig. 172 Embryo bed roll from plastic tube.

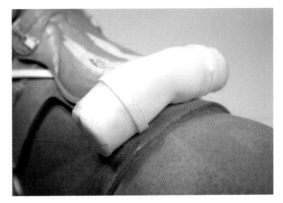

Fig. 173 New straps and buckles are added.

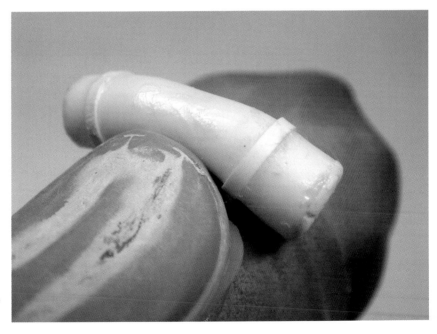

Fig. 174 New bedding roll in place on saddle.

pouches, shown in Figs. 175 to 179, were used to carry everything from food to ammunition. They were manufactured from a heavy (5mm thick) gauge of well-cured leather, tanned especially for use in the Tropics and sub-Saharan Africa. They are made from the oblong-section pouches provided with the kit. First, trim off the heavy surface detail, until the pouches resemble the shapes of those shown in Figs. 175 and 176, filling and sanding where necessary as you go. The raised edges are then added, as shown in Fig. 177 – be very careful to

hold the strips in place whilst the glue sets properly. The flaps (10-thou sheet) are then cemented in place (Fig. 178).

Fig. 179 shows the final shaping of the flap edges, filling, and the shape of the undulations in the flaps. This state would result from the leather being wet, sagging on to the pouch edge below it, and then re-drying in the sun. We replicate this by coating the underside of the flap in model cement, then carefully pressing it down on to the pouch proper while it dries. The brass press-studs are then added, as shown.

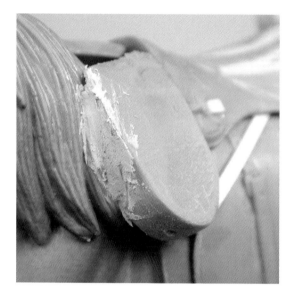

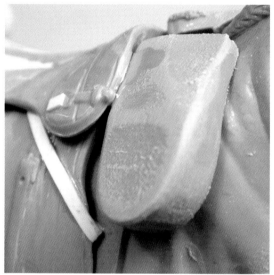

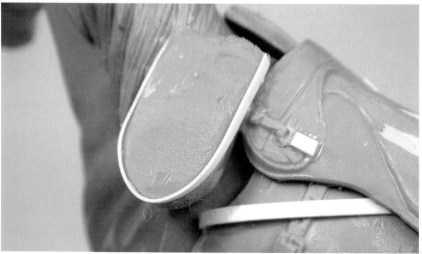

ABOVE LEFT: *Fig. 175 Leather equipment pouch in place on saddle side.*

ABOVE: *Fig. 176 Right pouch for food and ammunition.*

LEFT: *Fig. 177 Raised edge fluting from plastic strip.*

Fig. 178 Leather flaps in place on pouch tops.

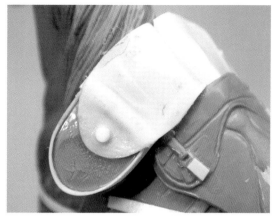

Fig. 179 Press-studs added from plastic rod.

Mounted Infantryman

The infantry officers of the Lancashire Fusiliers Regiment became sought-after targets for Boer Kommando snipers. As a consequence, the minimum amount of insignia was worn whilst on patrol. Indeed, anything that identified their rank was increasingly discarded as the guerilla war dragged on. Officers came to carry rifles such as the Lee Metford, bolt-action type shown in the accompanying reference photographs, allowing them to resemble more the NCOs and 'other ranks' that they commanded.

Fig. 180 shows how the German belt buckle is removed. This can be achieved by judicious use of a Dremel-type tool, or a scalpel blade, via a gradual shaving method. If using the latter, trimming a little at a time is safer, and it is easier to control the outcome! Fig. 181 illustrates the removal of the outside lower pockets. Once again, the scalpel, or motorized drill/burr combination, is suitable, but you will need to go carefully, as this is not the thickest part of the moulding. If you do cause any nicks or scratches during this process, they can be filled and sanded very easily, and made good to the existing surface.

Fig. 180 Remove belt buckle carefully with scalpel blade.

Fig. 181 Remove pockets using scalpel and rough-grade emery paper.

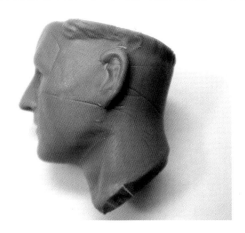

Fig. 182 Slice head top away with jigsaw.

Fig. 183 New position for head provided with kit.

At Fig. 182, the head-chopping commences! Once you have decided upon the angle at which the hat will sit, cut off the top of the head in an appropriate fashion with a fine-bladed jigsaw. Trim any unwanted, peripheral

Fig. 184 Check final stance for correct positioning of components.

burrs with a fresh scalpel blade. Fig. 183 shows the new position in which the head is fixed to the collar portion.

In Fig. 184 the stance of the figure is becoming apparent and in Fig. 185 it is beginning to resemble the finished article. His right arm is fitted into place with a little glue in order to assess the best position for it when assembly is complete. Before fitting, the recesses where the butt of the Sturmgewehr 44 weapon should fit (in the arm and body) are both filled with model putty, remembering to put in sufficient filler to create both the peaks and troughs of the emergent creases being created. In Fig. 186, the filler in the arm is beginning to take shape. Successive passes with progressively finer 'wet and dry' paper will reveal the true paths of the sleeve folds. The filling of the body–arm juncture takes place in Fig. 187, which shows the arm in situ on the torso – only to show correct alignment of the parts, one relative to the other. The filling/sanding should take place with the arm removed from the torso, to allow access to the side of the arm adjacent to the figure's body. Fig. 188 shows the final position of the left arm, which will hold the horse's bridle when the assembly is complete. Position this only when horse and figure are standing adjacent to one another on a flat surface (possibly on their diorama base). In this way you can assess the

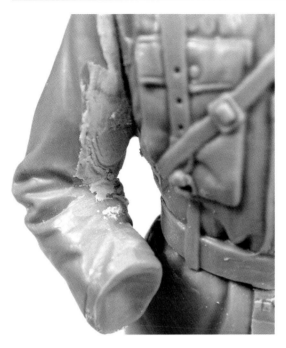

Fig. 185 Arm filling with model filler and glue combination.

Fig. 186 Sleeve folds are re-configured with scalpel and fine emery.

Fig. 187 Torso and arm joints before sanding.

Fig. 188 New position for raised left arm.

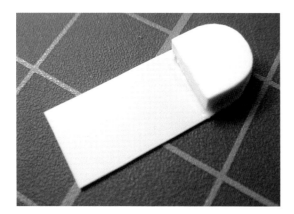

Fig. 189 Ammunition pouch preliminary cuts and folds.

Fig. 190 New flap folded in correct attitude.

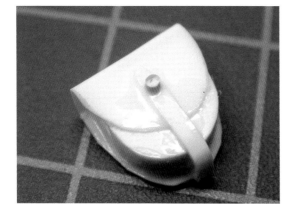

Fig. 191 Press-stud added from 2mm diameter plastic rod.

best position for the arm, when the reins on the horse have been cut to the correct length, to fit into the figure's left hand. The reins will be glued to the figure's hand only after the painting stage is completed. The horse and rider should be kept as sub-assemblies for that purpose.

Accoutrements

Fig. 189 shows the commencement of the fabrication of the leather pistol-ammunition holder which fits on to the Sam Browne-pattern belt. A short length of Evergreen strip measuring 5 × 8 × 7mm is cut from a suitable piece. One end should be rounded, as shown in the picture, using a stout-bladed knife and progressively finer grades of wet and dry paper, until the illustrated shape is achieved. In Fig. 190, the 15mm long strip added in Fig. 189 is rounded in the same way, and fixed in place, forming the flap cover to the pouch. The 2mm diameter press-stud is fitted in place carefully once the strap is affixed (*see* Fig. 191).

Fig. 192 shows the pistol holster, which is made in an identical manner to the ammunition holder, fixed in place on the Sam Browne. The telescope tube holder shown in Figs. 193 and 194 is manufactured in the same manner as the ammunition pouch. A 2.5cm length of 6mm diameter

Fig. 192 Pistol holster for Webley pistol.

Fig. 193 Telescope tube from suitable plastic tube length.

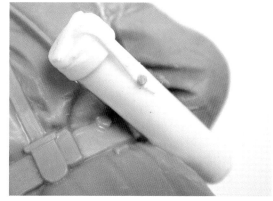

Fig. 194 Locking straps and retainers in place.

plastic tubing is used, with a 10mm length of 3mm wide strip forming the edge of the lid. The ends are sealed with circles cut from 20-thou sheet (one at 6mm, the other at 8mm). Straps are then added, as shown in Figs. 194 and 195, to complete the article. (Incidentally, the first recorded use of 'binoculars' on the battlefield was by British officers at the Siege of Mafeking, who borrowed ladies' opera glasses in order to see the Boers approaching from a distance!)

In Fig. 196, the moustache is shown in place. It is best to consult the accompanying reference photographs before you cut this item, from 20-thou plastic strip, as they came in all shapes and sizes, waxed and un-waxed! Texture can be added using the point of a scalpel, or a strand of your own hair.

Fig. 195 Cross-strapping to Sam Browne belt added.

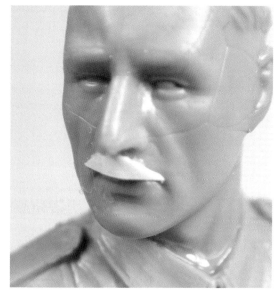

Fig. 196 Rough-cut moustache from 20-thou plastic sheet.

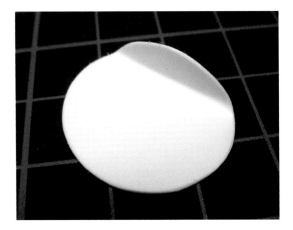

Fig. 197 Brim edge turned up rough-rider style.

Fig. 198 Crown made up of plastic laminations.

The brim of the hat measures 2cm (1in) in diameter. Fig. 197 shows the 20-thou disc cut out, and the side brim turned up (using thumb and forefinger). This will stay in place once it is glued to the side of the crown. Figs. 198 to 200 show the genesis of the crown, from laminations of 60-thou sheet, cut to shape with reference to the accompanying diagram. Finally, the crown should be sanded and formed into the shape shown in Figs. 201 and 202. These pictures also show the disposition of the hat-band, which should be glued into place after the side brim has been fixed.

In Figs. 203 and 204, the scratch-built Mauser pistol (a captured Boer weapon), and the 20-thou × 2mm reins can be seen in place. The Mauser can be built easily and completely from plastic strip and rod, using the accompanying diagram and reference photographs.

Fig. 199 Crown starts to take on final shape.

Fig. 200 Hat shaped and sanded to suit.

Fig. 201 Hat position and band from front.

Fig. 202 Hat-band position viewed from rear.

Fig 203 Mauser pistol added but not yet glued in place.

Fig. 204 Reins added from plastic strip.

PAINTING

Airbrushing the figure and horse is not as difficult as you might imagine. If you are new to airbrushing, you may want to practise a little on a flat surface before you wade in to a job like this, always remembering that, if you are not happy with your results at any stage, you can always airbrush over them! I use an Iwata HPSB airbrush, which, after 30-odd years of airbrushing, is by far the best that I have used. Your choice of airbrush is a highly personal one, and its purchase is one of the most important decisions you will make as a modeller. Always try to buy well, remembering that expensive does not necessarily mean better. Handle as many as possible before making your decision, as this is an item that you will use, hopefully, for many years to come. The HPSB is ideal in this case, being capable of drawing a line as narrow as 2mm! You will also be using a variety of conventional paintbrushes. The degree to which you use them will be up to you.

The Figure

Once assembly of your model is complete, the usual course is to cover it in an undercoat of a neutral colour, such as pale grey. This model is already moulded in a pale grey colour, so you may not need an undercoat. Paint coats build up gradually, and in extreme circumstances, can begin to obscure moulded detail, to a greater or lesser degree. Two or maybe three coats of a particular colour – for example, flesh tones – are permissible, but any more will cause the facial creases to fill in, and detail to become 'softer'. Use your judgement carefully. Try to keep your paint coats thin – when mixing Tamiya and Lifecolor acrylics, as used on this project, you will probably be guided towards a mix of 60 to 70 per cent paint, to 30 to 40 per cent acrylic thinner. This will allow you to get a good coverage while allowing freedom of flow through the airbrush.

In Figs. 205 and 206, the flesh tones are gradually being built up, as is the shadowing of the slightly darker tones below the eyelids, hat

Fig. 205 Flesh tones are added via airbrush.

Fig. 206 Gradual shading with various darker tones.

Fig. 207 Hair detail added with fine paintbrush.

Fig. 208 Paint in flesh and eye details first.

brim, nose and cheekbones. The progressive shading used on the flesh tones and clothing creases becomes easy (with practice). In Fig. 207, the details are beginning to appear, as the eyes and hair/eyebrows are picked out with a fine sable brush (size 00), loaded with Tamiya Dark Brown. Fig. 208 shows the benefit of painting the flesh first! It is always preferable to paint the colour around the collar and cuffs of a uniform, as it 'contains' the flesh and helps add to the illusion that the clothes are being worn over the skin (Fig. 209). I use a No.3 or 4 brush at this stage.

The Khaki colour is always a bone of contention among figure modellers, the exact hue being one of the great 'unknowables' of military history. Hundreds of thousands, if not millions, of uniforms were manufactured from cloth woven and dyed in hundreds of mills (most of them in Lancashire), so shades and sometimes even colours inevitably varied. The Lancashire Fusiliers' museum at Bury in Lancashire possesses several of the type, including one

Fig. 209 Uniform is hand painted with khaki mix.

Fig. 210 Cap badge is added and painted with suitable silver/brass shades.

Fig. 211 Shading coats are now added.

Fig. 212 Dry-brush creases with paler tone of original uniform colour.

Fig. 213 Rear view before details are added.

complete uniform for a boy soldier of the time – each one is different in colour and cut. I have used the boy soldier's one as a colour reference, as it was never issued, and has stayed hidden in a drawer for over a hundred years; it is therefore an invaluable reference! A further consideration is that uniforms become faded and generally 'tired' while their wearers are on campaign. The figure in this model is from the officer cadre, and modelled at a point in time several weeks after his arrival in South Africa – about the time when the battalion reached the Transvaal – and as such he is still looking rather dapper.

Fig. 210 shows the cap badge in place (manufactured with reference to the accompanying photograph), and the final uniform's coat of paint almost dried. Of course,

any cap badge of a regiment operating in South Africa would be equally suitable, as this uniform type was common to all. To begin shading (Fig. 211), turn the airbrush to its finest setting, and move in as close as is practicable. Fill the airbrush with a mixture of your base (khaki) and a small amount of black paint. The ratio is up to you, but be careful to spray only the underside of clothing creases – try not to get carried away. Fig. 212 shows the dry-brushing of the crease highlights with a mixture of the base khaki colour and white (roughly 50–50, but choose according to the finish you prefer). These steps should be completed before strap and accoutrement details are added, as illustrated in Fig. 213. The straps and accoutrements will require careful

Fig. 214 Strap details added for bridle assembly.

Fig. 215 Canteen and bed roll are now painted and detailed.

detail-painting with a No.1 or 2 brush. Don't worry too much if you think that your brush is a little on the large side, as long as it comes to a sharp point. A No.4 or 5 brush can be suitable, and will hold much more paint, enabling you to paint for longer, so that you do not have to keep breaking off and then re-focusing your concentration.

The Lancashire Fusiliers in South Africa in 1900 were raised from local Lancashire militia, and some would say that they had something to prove to the regular army units – hence the shiny boots! In Fig. 216 the blacking of the boots has been achieved by mixing black gloss and matt acrylics in the ratio of 70–30, gloss to matt. This gives a very realistic finish once it has been thinned with 40 per cent thinners, which enables the mixture's free flow through the airbrush. The Mauser pistol (Fig. 217) was brush-painted in the same black that was mixed for the boots, and then dry-brushed with silver. The strap details were added, in Fig. 218, with reference to items found in the Fusiliers' archive.

Fig. 216 Polished boots are picked out with gloss black.

Fig. 217 Mauser pistol dry-brushed silver to accentuate worn breech mechanism.

Fig. 218 Further strap detail to rear of figure.

The Horse

Once it has been adapted, the horse has a quite placid appearance; perhaps, after a long day in the Veld, he has just had enough! The procedure for painting is very similar to that used for the figure, except that the highlights are added via the airbrush, in order to preserve the smooth texture of the horse's coat at this scale. In Fig. 219, the base coat of red-brown has been applied via a suitable aerosol. Figs. 220 and 221 show the addition of the darker shading coat of dark red-brown to the underside of the muscle creases, and the careful brush-painting of the saddle, blanket and harness detail. Fig. 222 shows dry-brushed detail of white/cream colours around the fetlocks, nose and leather-work.

The highlights are airbrushed (along the raised portions of the muscles) with the airbrush on its finest setting. This will bring out the very fine texture of the horse's coat, and allow you to practise your skills with the airbrush on an area that is very visible on the finished model. Resist the temptation (which is great) to overdo it. If you do, you can put more shadow back in later (Fig. 223). Fig. 224 shows the results of the white dry-brush coat applied to the mane and tail. These are perfectly acceptable areas of the kit, but you may want to 'tease' them with a soldering iron, in order to

Fig. 219 Base colour applied to horse.

enhance the 'hairiness'. Pick out the harness metalwork details carefully, with a No.1 brush, and a suitable silver or brass colour from Alclad, or similar. The horse's eyes should be a high-gloss black, with a tiny white gloss highlight – a good look into the eyes of a local horse should give you some inspiration.

Fig. 220 Shadow detail added via airbrush coats.

Fig. 221 Saddle and blanket initial paint coats in place.

LEFT: *Fig. 222 White blaze to horse's forehead.*

RIGHT: *Fig. 223 Flank highlights added with paintbrush and airbrush.*

ABOVE: *Fig. 224 Mane and tail details – see reference shots.*

RIGHT: *Fig. 225 Eye detail and highlight added.*

This is a great introduction to figure conversions in a larger scale. The kit concerned is cost-effective and user-friendly, but any figure and any horse could be used to equally good effect, and to represent many of the regiments that served throughout the Empire at this time. Figs. 226 and 227 were taken 'on location' on the hills above the new National Museum of the Royal Regiment of Fusiliers (the five Fusilier Regiments combined), in Bury, Lancashire. (The battalions destined for South Africa were trained in this area.) Without the help of the museum's curator, Lieutenant-Colonel Mike Glover, and his staff, this project would not have been possible, and the finished diorama depicting the battalion's arrival in the Johannesburg area, and including this conversion, can now be seen at the museum.

OPPOSITE: *Fig. 226 Training on Holcombe Hill, Lancashire.*

OPPOSITE, INSET: *Fig. 227 Sepia tone applied via Adobe Photoshop programme.*

LANCASHIRE FUSILIERS
FURTHER REFERENCE

This section will help you to create optional pieces of kit, and vital detail additions to your conversion.

Fig. 229 Helmet badge detail (left side only).

ABOVE: *Fig. 228 A real-life Fusilier, John Scotson, sporting a genuine 'puggaree'-style cork and canvas helmet from 1899.*

RIGHT: *Fig. 230 Lee Metford .303 rifle. Close-up of the breech, trigger and magazine details.*

BELOW: *Fig. 231 Lee Metford .303 rifle. This model dates from 1898, and was the precursor to the famous Lee Enfield range of weapons.*

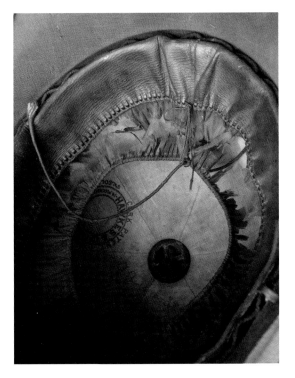

Fig. 232 Helmet interior.

Fig. 233 Fusiliers in Natal, 1899.

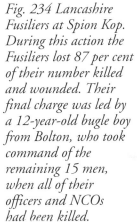

Fig. 234 Lancashire Fusiliers at Spion Kop. During this action the Fusiliers lost 87 per cent of their number killed and wounded. Their final charge was led by a 12-year-old bugle boy from Bolton, who took command of the remaining 15 men, when all of their officers and NCOs had been killed.

Fig. 235 Fusiliers mounted infantry being drilled at Wellington Barracks, Bury, prior to departure for South Africa.

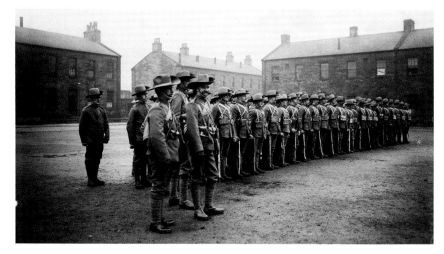

Fig. 236 Officers to the fore.

Fig. 237 Excellent equipment detail shot.

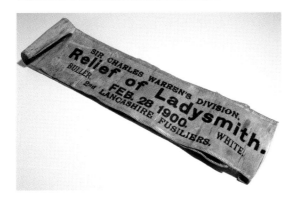

ABOVE: *Fig. 238 'Relief of Ladysmith' armband. This event definitely struck a chord back in England; my grandmother still talked about it up to her death in 1990, aged 100!*

RIGHT: *Fig. 239 Typical 'rough-rider' uniform whilst on campaign.*

BELOW: *Fig. 240 Lancashire Fusiliers at rest. Note the 'Other Ranks'-pattern belt buckle, and equipment by Slade-Wallace.*

ABOVE: *Fig. 241 'Other Ranks' badge – lightweight, and more durable than the Shako badge (3cm high).*

RIGHT: *Fig. 242 The Lancashire Fusiliers Busby/Shako plate from 1890. This item was often worn on campaign as an alternative to the 'Other Ranks' badge (5.5cm high).*

Fig. 243 Box artwork for DML's Wehrmacht mounted infantryman, the model upon which this conversion is based.

CHAPTER 5

Fusilier John Lynn VC

THE HISTORY

John Lynn VC, DCM, received his Victoria Cross for a protracted act of courage at Ypres on 2 May 1915. Bravery often begets an act that takes place on the spur of the moment, when an ordinary person does something quite extraordinary, often without pause to consider the consequences. John Lynn's actions redefined courage in as much as his VC was earned over the course of hours.

The German forces in the Ypres-salient sector had planned their attack as part of an overall strategy to dislodge the British regiments from their well-prepared positions, thus collapsing a huge 'sack'-shaped salient in their defences. The trench system held by 2nd Battalion Lancashire Fusiliers was a well-sited one, with the machine-gun sections having excellent fields of fire. To negate this advantage the Germans initially deployed an artillery bombardment firing high-explosive rounds, which subsequently gave way to phosgene gas munitions being launched once the wind was found to be blowing toward the Fusiliers' trenches. Although rudimentary gas masks were available, they were not yet in widespread use. John Lynn and his fellow Fusiliers had only handkerchiefs and rags soaked in their own urine to give scant protection from a gas that literally boiled and seared the lungs when inhaled.

Pre-siting a field of fire for the Vickers-Maxim gun meant that, as the German infantry advanced en masse upon the 'LFs' position, John Lynn and his gun team were able to keep up a sustained level of fire during the initial stages. Amid the yells and screams of the Germans wounded and killed by the 700 rounds per minute scything the tops of the long grass on the left and right and in the centre, the remaining Infantry of Duke Albrecht of Wurtemburg's 4th Army were forced to crawl forwards to make their attack. Lynn and his mates were now 25 minutes into the engagement. Two men lay shot dead in the bottom of the trench, whilst others lay writhing in the agony of a death often compared to slow drowning. Lynn was struggling too and, against a hail of well-aimed rifle fire, dragged the awesome weight of the Vickers gun and its ammunition belts up and on to the parapet of the trench, to better hit the crawling and crouching Germans.

Private John Lynn stayed at his post, firing continuously for over an hour, until the gas was almost completely dissipated and the remaining Germans had retreated. His selfless courage in the face of overwhelming odds had put paid completely to the German attack. He had fought latterly, single-handed, and his actions had prevented the collapse of the British defensive line in that sector. He died in a casualty clearing station behind the line the following day, of the effects of gas inhalation. His contribution to victory was so significant as to be mentioned in despatches written by General French himself.

CREATING THE MODEL

Although this is the story of John Lynn's VC action, making the model has much in common with the identically clad and equipped soldiers of the British Army, and many others, throughout the Great War. The venerable scale of 54mm, or 1/32nd scale, was chosen for this subject as the excellent Multipose figures from Airfix convert readily into soldiers wearing uniforms of the Great War period. Unfortunately, there are still relatively few mainstream manufacturers willing to venture back as far as 1915, so we are left to our own devices! This diorama depicts the early part of the action wherein the gun team are just beginning to feel the effects of the gas inhalation. Their stances were chosen accordingly.

You will need one each of 'Japanese Infantry', 'British Infantry' and '8th Army' packs from the Airfix Multipose range of 1/32nd scale figures. You may wish to scratch-build your own Vickers-Maxim gun, or use the excellent offering from Belgian company Resicast. This machine gun is billed as 1/35th scale, but, according to my calculations, and by substituting the tripod legs for ones made from plastic rod (3mm longer than the originals), it scales out at 1/32nd! The barrel shown in Figs. 244 and 245 is 4mm longer than the original

kit barrel, and is fitted with a new muzzle, or 'spout'. The breech mechanism is made 1mm deeper by the addition of a sliver of plastic strip added to the underside. The effect is very pleasing and, short of scratch-building, or tracking down the rare Airfix polythene 'British Infantry Support Team' Vickers from the 1970s, it provides an excellent solution.

Figure One

John Lynn VC was a young man of average build for the time. Being from a Lancashire mill town meant that he and his mates were all a little shorter than the national average. The choice of legs from the Japanese infantry pack in Fig. 246 is therefore a fortuitous one, as Second World War Japanese folk were also on the short side, in comparison with their European counterparts. The Japanese troops in the Second World War were also still wearing gaiters above their boots, so this kit replicates well the British boys' First World War leg wear, once the cross-strapping has been carefully removed with a craft knife. The separate right and left legs being cut in Fig. 247 were needed to achieve the kneeling position in Figs. 248 and 249. Both sets of legs should be cut, as shown, with a fine-bladed jigsaw, and the resulting burrs removed with a scalpel and fine emery paper (along with the mould-lines). Figs. 250 and 251 illustrate the stance achieved once

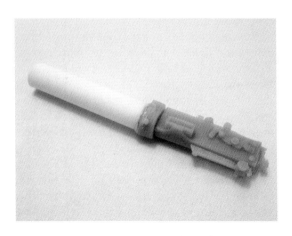

Fig. 244 New Maxim-Vickers barrel in place.

Fig. 245 Muzzle detail and fore sight.

Fig. 246 Careful choice of legs is necessary.

Fig. 247 Initial leg surgery takes place.

the torso is in place. This is chosen from the British Infantry set, as the Battle-Dress short blouson is an excellent representation of the top part of the 1914 Service Dress uniform. In fact the latter gave birth to the former due to shortages of raw materials during the Second World War. It was found that the square footage of material used during the manufacture of the First World War item was reduced by one-third when making the 'BD' jacket from 1938 onwards.

In Figs. 252 and 253 the 'wrap-around' takes place! To re-create the 'below waist' portion of the First World War vintage uniform, cut a piece of 80 gsm white paper using your circle cutter, set to an 8cm radius for what will become the lower edge. Re-set the radius, reducing it by 8mm to achieve the semi-circular strip of paper shown in Fig. 252. These measurements will naturally change if you use leg/torso combinations that are different from those shown here. A little experimentation may be

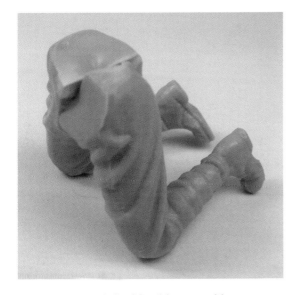

Fig. 248 Front left of final leg assembly.

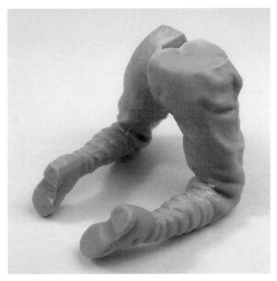

Fig. 249 Rear of leg assembly – note stance.

Fig. 250 Torso in place atop leg assembly.

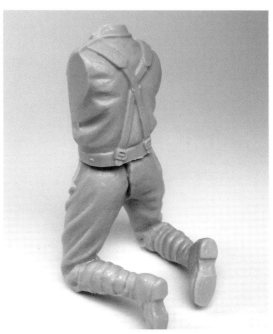

Fig. 251 Stance must be checked at every stage of construction.

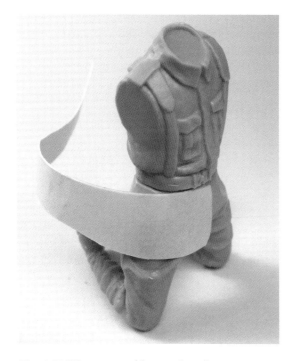

Fig. 252 Wrap-around lower edge of service tunic.

Fig. 253 Lower jacket edge from left rear.

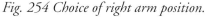

Fig. 254 Choice of right arm position.

Fig. 255 View of assembly from front left.

necessary. Figs. 254 and 255 illustrate the slight forward lean of the figure, necessarily adopted when kneeling to fire the Vickers gun, whilst also attempting to gain a little height to better survey the field of fire. The choice of torso should be made in order to correspond with the attitude required in the final assembly of the complete figure. The arms should likewise be chosen to best suit John Lynn's purpose. In the case shown here he is gripping the firing handle, while, when the left arm is added, also adjusting the folded-down distance-sight atop the gun's breech. The 'wrap-around' should be fitted to the right upper leg area first (Fig. 252) with super-glue. This will set very quickly due to the absorption properties of the paper. Wind the paper around the upper legs, as shown in Figs. 253 and 254, placing a tiny blob of glue at each of the three remaining points of the compass. Ensure that the top edge of the paper engages snugly below, and touches the line made by the torso's belt. Add the lower jacket pocket flaps, as shown in Fig. 255, made from tiny slivers of the remaining paper.

The Lancashire Fusiliers, in common with many regiments in the line in 1915, were wearing the '08 pattern webbing, which had five small bullet pouches at each side of the belt buckle. Some regiments were still wearing the Slade-Wallace issue webbing of the Boer War period, and its replicas produced in leather during the early period of the First World War; you will need to consult reference material where appropriate. As the cross-strapping is well represented on the torso already, it is possible to replicate the pouches for the '08 webbing by cutting down the 'BD' bullet pouches supplied with both British sets of figures (*see* Fig. 257). Be careful to cut with the edge of the scalpel blade closest to the handle, in order to apply maximum pressure safely during the cut. Trim the pouch tabs and bottom edges to complete the transformation. You can also trim a little off the rear of the resultant smaller pouch if it is to be depicted devoid of bullet clips. Fig. 258 shows the stance check, complete with the Vickers.

RIGHT: *Fig. 256 Check assembly of limbs against rear of weapon.*

BELOW: *Fig. 257 Configuration of new-type bullet pouch.*

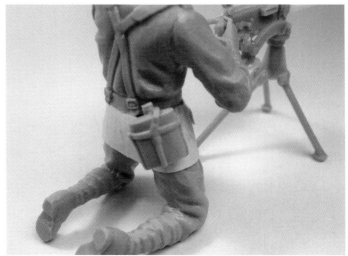

Fig. 258 John Lynn VC in position.

Figure Two

The construction of the second figure, by necessity, shares a good deal of its manufacturing process with the first figure, as the relevant pictures show. Bear in mind that the body parts selection will need to be guided by the function you choose for the finished figure in the diorama. Mine is feeding the ammunition, but he could easily be modelled knelt up, clearing a stoppage in the gun's firing mechanism.

I chose a pair of Japanese legs in the prone position, along with a British torso and suitable arms from a figure lying down and firing (Figs. 259 and 260). Fig. 261 shows the final body assembly, after all mould-lines have been removed with a scalpel blade and fine emery paper. In Fig. 262 the 'wrap-around' of the jacket's lower half is once more achieved with the use of radius-cut 80 gsm paper and super-glue (Fig. 263). The small pack and canteen are added in Fig. 264, and the whole sequence and 'sit' of the figures, and their interaction, is depicted in Figs. 265 and 266.

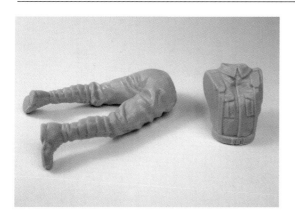

Fig. 259 Selection of relevant body parts for second figure.

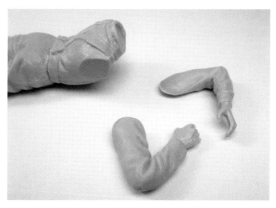

Fig. 260 Arm selection should suit attitude of prone figure.

Fig. 261 Assembly of parts should ensure correct 'sit' of figure.

Fig. 262 Wrap-around of lower jacket portion in place.

Fig. 263 Jacket finished and side pack in place.

Fig. 264 Canteen final position with correct angle for full vessel.

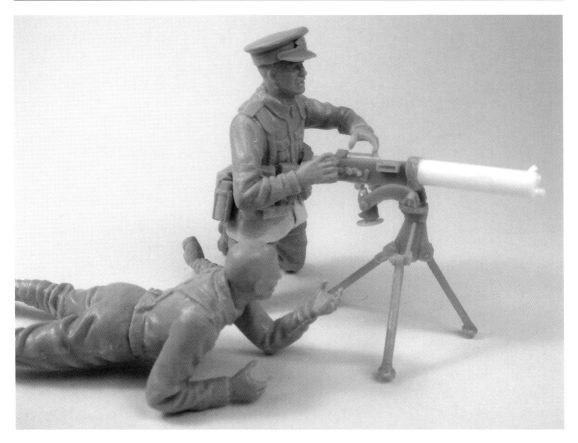

ABOVE: *Fig. 265 Final group position front left view.*

LEFT: *Fig. 266 John Lynn leans into the firing position.*

Figure Three

This lieutenant is beginning to feel the effects of the phosgene gas. The process of leg/torso selection, and the addition of the lower part of the General Service jacket depicted in Figs. 267 to 273, are the same as for the previous two figures, and an easy process to follow via the photographs. There is one note to be made, referring to Fig. 271 – the bottom part of the jacket (paper portion) is shown slightly apart at the front, following the attitude of the legs. Use the reference pictures here, along with your own collected research in order to depict more accurately the desired position. In Fig. 273, the canteen is angled slightly downwards. This would most likely occur due to the effect of gravity on a full water bottle. An empty one would not necessarily hang so far down, as the friction between its fabric and that of the tunic would hinder its movement.

The head in place on the figure in Fig. 274 comes from the Hornet range, and is sporting a haircut suitable for an officer of the period. The choice of a 1/35th scale head (nominally) might seem an unusual one, but you must bear in mind that people have different-sized body

Fig. 267 Careful selection of relevant leg components.

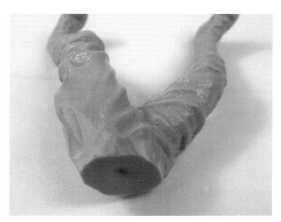

Fig. 268 Hips are carefully carved to correct proportion.

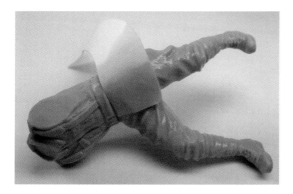

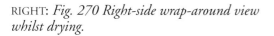

ABOVE: *Fig. 269 Left-side view oblique.*

RIGHT: *Fig. 270 Right-side wrap-around view whilst drying.*

Fig. 271 Jacket lower portion gap at front.

Fig. 272 Side pack in position on figure's left side.

components! Although basically similar, all humans differ in detail, as should your models. Some choices when intermixing scaled components are wrong, and look wrong. You should always, though, in the best traditions of the British Army, be willing to exercise your judgement and use your own initiative at all times. If it looks right, it usually is right. The hand surgery in Fig. 275 is necessary, in order

to swivel the wrist so that it comes into a more natural position to be holding the urine-soaked rag, which protects the soldier against some of the effects of the gas (Fig. 276). Figs. 277 and 278 show the stance check, and the addition of the cap from the 8th Army set. Finally, in Figs. 279 and 280, the interaction of the figures is checked before the diorama is built.

Fig. 273 Canteen position on lower right side of webbing belt.

Fig. 274 New head added from the Hornet range.

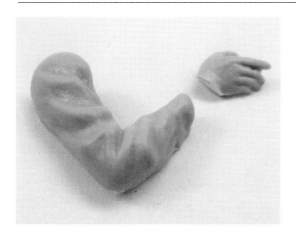

ABOVE: *Fig. 275 Elementary hand surgery to change wrist angle.*

RIGHT: *Fig. 276 New hand position achieved after arm is fixed in place.*

BELOW LEFT: *Fig. 277 Rear right-side view.*

BELOW RIGHT: *Fig. 278 Field service cap now in left hand.*

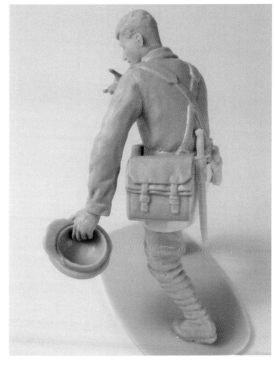

LEFT: *Fig. 279 All figures are now checked for interaction.*

BELOW: *Fig. 280 Rear view of final figure positions.*

FURTHER REFERENCE

ABOVE: *Fig. 281 Victoria Cross for extreme gallantry.*

RIGHT: *Fig. 282 1914 service cap detail.*

Fig. 283 John Lynn in action, from an original by the author.

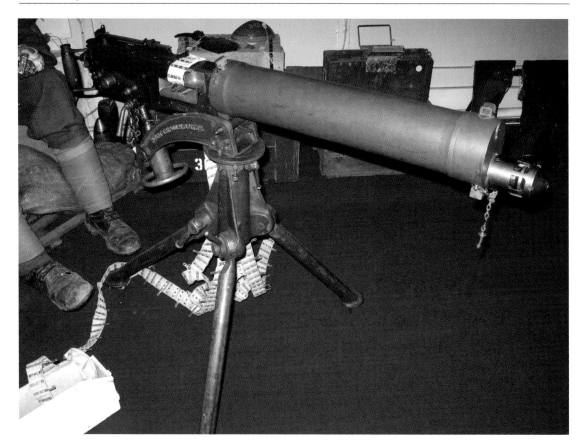

Fig. 284 Front right of Vickers gun.

Fig. 285 Vickers gun right rear mounting bracket.

Fig. 286 Vickers-Maxim firing grip detail.

Fig. 287 Pivot mounting for traverse of weapon.

Fig. 288 Fusiliers' Lewis gun team at practice.

Fig. 289 John Lynn's gun section at practice, Ypres 1915.

Fig. 290 Lancashire Fusiliers with later-type Vickers gun in 1917.

Fig. 291 Lancashire Fusilier in Service Dress, 1915. (Illustration by the author.)

DIORAMA

RIGHT: *Fig. 292 A sustained cyclic rate of 700 rounds per minute.*

BELOW: *Fig. 293 The scene at the start of the action.*

Fig. 294 Detail of Vickers-Maxim from rear right.   *Fig. 295 Officer present, though stooping!*

Fig. 296 Early effects of the phosgene gas are difficulty in breathing and dizziness.

CHAPTER 6

Russian Tank Riders

THE HISTORY

At the height of the Siege of Leningrad, in the Russia of 1942, the peasant army of the Soviet Union considered themselves to be in a state of 'Deep War'. They had fought thus far to rid their homeland of the German invaders for no pay, a situation that would persist until the war's end. The KV 5 Heavy Assault tank shown here was a prototype – no one today even knows whether it saw combat in those dark days. I chose to build it to illustrate the desperate plight of the poorly supported Russians. The Red Army was not as blessed as the Germans, or indeed the rest of the Allies, with a vast array of infantry-carrying vehicles (many of which, in the case of the Germans, were horse-drawn). Armies such as 1st Ukrainian Tank Army were just that – armies composed mainly of tanks, and tens of thousands of tank riders.

CREATING THE MODEL

Hobby stores now stock quite a variety of tank-rider figure kits which are beautifully cast and detailed. You can always arrange proprietary figures alongside each other, but, in order to make them interact in precisely the way you need them to for a particular diorama, you may feel the need to convert.

  The heroes in this model are from one of the relieving units flooding into Leningrad to help lift the siege. They are eager, well equipped and spoiling for a fight. The components were selected from the now-venerable Russian Assault Infantry kit by Tamiya, the Soviet Infantry Tank Riders from Dragon, and Hand to Hand Fight 1941–42 from Master Box. The crowning glory is the individually sculpted heads from the legendary Hornet range of products. There is nothing wrong with other manufacturers' head components, but the Hornet sculpting is less 'generic' in its rendering of facial features and expressions, in fact sometimes it is downright spooky! Tank-rider kit figures are often just riding, but you may prefer to have guys who are reacting, jumping off, and shooting!

Fig. 297 New Hornet head in place.

Fig. 298 Glue deposits to be removed with scalpel blade.

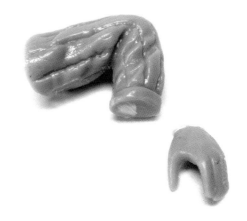

Fig. 299 Sever left hand with scalpel.

Figure One

There is no shortage of extra weapons in figure kits today, so you can mix and match as you see fit. Imagine that you are that tank rider – what would you carry, and how would you react? Take figure 'D' from the Dragon kit for customization (Fig. 297). Assemble the figure using all but the head and left arm. Before assembly, make sure that all of the mould-lines (light on this figure) are carefully removed with a fresh scalpel blade. Remove the relevant Hornet head from its casting block with a pair of very fine snips, being careful to hold on to it tightly. A room-wide carpet search is not much fun! Be careful to cut as close to the casting block as possible, so that you can then place the head close to the neck of the figure's torso whilst you decide exactly the angle at which your final cut should be made. This will ensure that you have complete control of its final position. Place the super-glue on the figure's neck, and the head/neck on to the glue (Fig. 297).

Fig. 298 shows the rear of the figure's neck/head juncture. The residual glue/activator has overflowed the joint, nestling in the creases of the comrade's Telogreika M1941 jacket. This is easily rectified, as the deposit can be removed with the tip of a scalpel blade, and some very fine emery paper. In Fig. 299, the hand is severed from the figure's left arm and rotated through 90

Fig. 300 Rotate hand to accept weapon.

degrees, before being glued back into place on the wrist stub. This will ensure that he can hold the Moisin-Nagant rifle realistically, as opposed to the Degtyarev machine gun supplied for him in the kit (Figs. 300 and 301). In Fig. 302, he is on top of the tank's turret, nearly 13ft (4m) from the ground. His body language betrays a degree of trepidation.

Fig. 301 Add weapon, Moisin-Nagant rifle.

Figure Two

The second figure is 'G' from the Tamiya Russian Assault Infantry set, and his stance is perfect for a man in charge. In Fig. 303, the obligatory mould-line trimming has already taken place, and the right arm has been modified. The kit arm (component code G3), is pointing outwards at 180 degrees to the torso. The arm needs to be pointing at about 120 degrees, and a little trimming at the shoulder, and a vertical incision, will result in the position in Fig. 303. The new head is a Hornet item, with mouth open, screaming orders. Figs. 304 and 305 show the correct angle, and the point at which to cut the neck. In Figs. 306 and 307, the stance is checked, and the head position reviewed in relation to the position of the arm. Looking at real people and the way in which their limbs move, one relative to the other, will be very useful. There are

Fig. 302 Figure in position atop KV5 turret.

Fig. 304 Selection of new head from the Hornet range.

Fig. 303 Chosen new arm in position.

Fig. 305 Angle of initial cut is crucial. Leave enough neck to trim.

ABOVE: Fig. 306 Critical stance check at this juncture.

RIGHT: Fig. 307 Final position is selected for the new head.

plenty of books on anatomy in the libraries, and other relevant reference all around you. Fig. 308 shows the left arm (d4) after surgery. The hand is to be rotated to the attitude shown in Fig. 309, to facilitate the more convincing position needed to hold the magazine of the sub-machine gun. In Fig. 310 the haversack is added, and Fig. 311 shows the finally checked stance. Remember, all of your conversions will be slightly different from those shown here. The best way to model is for yourself – if other people also like your work, that is a bonus.

ABOVE: *Fig. 308 Left hand and arm are separated.*

RIGHT: *Fig. 309 Selection of final stance position.*

Fig. 310 Rear left view of upper torso.

Fig. 311 Close-up of upper torso.

Figure Three

This man is 'tank jumping', rather than riding, as they usually are in proprietary kits. Fig. 312 shows the major component breakdown for the leg/boot area. The right leg is from figure 'A' (Dragon set) and is component A6. The left leg is from figure 'F' (part F5). The left boot has been removed with a stout knife blade, and a chamfer taken off (20 degrees), in order to facilitate the knee's extra articulation. The finished figure will use this leg to 'lever' himself from the tank's track guard.

Fig. 313 shows the components from Fig. 16 assembled. There is an obvious misalignment of the two legs at the waist portion, which helps the articulation of the left leg even further. Before attachment to the body, these legs must be levelled at the waist. Begin this by trimming, until roughly level, with a scalpel. Fix a piece of emery paper to the work-top, then, with the assembly thoroughly dry, hold the legs firmly, upside down, and work them gently up and down the paper. In Fig. 314, the upper torso (component C2) is in place, as is the filler, at the

Fig. 312 Critical choice of leg components.

knee joint and at the gap at the figure's waist. Fig. 315 shows the importance of filling every visible gap. At Fig. 316, the relevant Hornet head has been selected, and the previously outlined 'surgery' has taken place – taking close note of the angle selected for the cut.

Fig. 317 shows the figure's extra 'leverage' in place. Tank riders would often sit on their small haversacks for the sake of comfort on long

Fig. 313 Trim waist once legs are assembled.

Fig. 314 Check torso position relative to legs.

Fig. 315 All gaps must be closed with filler.

journeys. Fortunately, this helps this fellow over the raised lip at the edge of the track guard. In Fig. 318 the left arm from figure 'A' has been selected (A3), and before the arm can set finally, the assembly is offered into place on the tank, and duly adjusted (Fig. 319). In Fig. 320, the figure is checked from the front. In Fig. 321 the chap is looking complete.

The sub-machine gun is a heavy item in reality, and would have its own momentum when wielded in this way. The figure grips the weapon at the best point to 'retain' it! Whenever you are able, take a trip to your local museum. Make arrangements to handle and photograph the weapons, then yourself, or a friend, holding them (under supervision). This

ABOVE: *Fig. 316 Be careful to select the correct angle for the neck cut.*

RIGHT: *Fig. 317 Extra leverage is required to exit the tank's fender.*

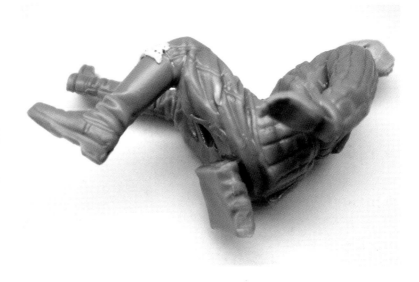

Fig. 318 New left arm component is selected.

Fig. 319 Test model figure in place on tank.

Fig. 320 Check attitude from all angles.

Fig. 321 Completed figure before painting.

will impart a high degree of realism to your model, and help you avoid modelling average-sized men (or women) firing a German MG 42 from the shoulder. I was disappointed to see this replicated on an otherwise excellent diorama. I could barely lift the weapon to my waist, let alone fire it like a rifle!

Figs. 322, 323 and 324 show the figure from different angles. Always check all of these, as a figure can look stunning from the front and much less believable from the rear viewpoint. Fig. 325 shows the final check with the figure in place on the tank. Fig. 326 shows the figure once the final sanding and tidying has taken place.

Fig. 322 Rear left side of completed figure.

Fig. 323 Front left-side attitude checked.

Fig. 324 Rear right side of figure checked.

Fig. 325 Test of completed figure on tank side.

Fig. 326 Final sanding and finishing takes place.

Fig. 327 Figure selected from the DML set.

Figure Four

Figs. 327 to 330 show the fourth figure, 'E' in the Dragon set. This man is concerned for the welfare of his comrade (Figure Three), and illustrates a good example of the axiom 'If it ain't broke, don't fix it!' As a result, figure 'E' is assembled as per the Dragon instructions, once the mould-lines have been intricately trimmed away. Before the kit head is fixed into place, the neck must be chamfered slightly at the 'Adam's apple' portion, in order that the chap can look downwards. The arms are cannibalized from figure 'D' in the Tamiya Russian Assault Infantry set. Duly trimmed, they are glued in place, and the whole assembly is tested on the tank along with Figure Three, to assess their interaction (Fig. 331). The suitability and 'sit' of the figure are gauged in Fig. 332; now is the ideal time to move the arms, if necessary, before the model-glue sets.

Fig. 333 shows the PPSH 41 sub-machine gun in place. The muzzle end of the barrel has been drilled out with the point of a fine scalpel blade, using a rotating, circular motion repeated about five times. (For more on this

Fig. 328 Tamiya right arm (rear view).

Fig. 329 Both selected arms are now in place.

ABOVE: *Fig. 330 Always check figure under construction from all angles.*

RIGHT: *Fig. 331 Use other figures to assess accuracy of interaction.*

ABOVE: *Fig. 332 Check 'sit' of figure in situ on tank.*

Fig. 333 Carefully drill out muzzle of machine gun with a fine scalpel blade.

technique, see the DVD *Military Modelling and Conversions* from Crowood, where it is shown being used on a Sherman bow machine gun.) Always, in the case of figures, perform this drilling once the weapon is glued in place, and set. This gives you the whole figure to hold on to, thus keeping your fingers away from the rotating scalpel blade! In Fig. 334, a final positional check is done, while Fig. 335 shows how well the concern for his comrade is shown (helped in no small way by the expressions on the Hornet and Dragon faces).

ABOVE: *Fig. 334 Position check (left rear quarter).*

RIGHT: *Fig. 335 The final stance of the figures enhances the quality of their interaction.*

Figure Five

This figure is the first German, desperately attacking as his position is about to be overrun. This appears to be quite an extreme animation, yet is based closely on the relevant figure in the excellent Eastern Front, Kit 3, Hand-to-Hand Fight, from Master Box. This kit is quite a shock if you are used to endless streams of German figure models from the Far East, in that it combines two German and two Russian figures from World War Two, engaged in a desperate hand-to-hand fight.

Fig. 336 shows the leg halves cemented together slightly 'askew', in order to impart a slight stagger to the final figure, as if he has just been shot, in mid-run. The right boot has also been removed and chamfered to aid the illusion of staggering once it is glued in place. The waist is flattened off in the manner explained earlier, and Figs. 337 and 338 show the fillet in place,

Fig. 336 Removal of right-hand boot.

Fig. 337 Angled insert from 60-thou plastic sheet.

121

Fig. 338 Right-side view of angled waist insert.

Fig. 339 Final attitude of torso is achieved.

which will push the torso backwards, causing the back to arch. This fillet is a composite of two portions of 60-thou plastic sheet, cut to shape, then chamfered with a craft knife to achieve the shape and attitude shown in Fig. 339.

At Fig. 340 his arms are added and the new Hornet head is seen in place. Once more, the angle at which the neck is cut helps towards the 'extreme' nature of the final figure's position. The figure is checked once more for authenticity of attitude at Figs. 341 and 342, before the sanding of mould-lines, midriff additions, and the addition of his Panzerfaust (Fig. 343). Fig. 344 shows the paint applied.

Fig. 340 New Hornet head is now fixed in place.

Fig. 341 Check angles throughout your assembly sequence.

Fig. 342 Check and remove all mould-lines.

ABOVE: *Fig. 343 Panzerfaust anti-tank weapon is now added.*

RIGHT: *Fig. 344 Paint coats are applied by airbrush.*

Figure Six

This Russian figure is to be made to interact directly with the 'on guard' German bayonet figure from the MB set, and as such it is necessary to test his suitability for the role against the bayonet figure, once the German is built 'straight from the box'. Basing the Russian figure on the kit figure advancing with his entrenching tool makes life a good deal easier, and shows that it is always best to choose figures that are already in an attitude closest to that which you would like to model. In Fig. 345 the components that will make up the leg portions are carefully cut up. Figs. 346 and 347 illustrate the best positions to fix the legs in order to make it appear that this figure's advance has been suddenly arrested (with a bayonet). The tops of both boots are angled as in previous figures.

Fig. 348 illustrates the final attitude, before the addition of a Tamiya arm, which will hold the sub-machine gun. (Be careful when swapping arms, especially between figures of the same army, who happen to be wearing uniforms of different material, or have cuff details that are not quite right.) Fig. 349 shows the SMG added, whilst the previously severed left hand is rotated and glued back in place at the cuff in Fig. 350. Fig. 351 shows that the

Fig. 345 Careful selection of all leg components.

Fig. 346 New leg positions are now selected.

ABOVE: *Fig. 347 Standard check of leg stance from rear.*

RIGHT: *Fig. 348 Cuff details must match if using arms from different figures and manufacturers.*

ABOVE: *Fig. 349 The sub-machine gun is now added.*

ABOVE RIGHT: *Fig. 350 Careful positioning of hand after rotation of wrist joint.*

RIGHT: *Fig. 351 Check shoulder/torso joint for realistic angle.*

Fig. 352 Remove front portion of left boot.

Fig. 353 New position of foot front half.

right arm needs a few millimetres' adjustment upwards at the side of the torso.

In Fig. 352, the front half of the left boot has been amputated, and the inner edge chamfered. It is then re-glued in place (Fig. 353), so that the foot will rest more realistically on the floor.

With his new head in place, the figure is then observed from all angles (Figs. 354 to 357), in order that adjustments can be made, and the interaction of the figures assessed. In Fig. 358, the paint has been applied, with particular attention paid to the eye area.

Fig. 354 Assessment of figures' interaction.

Fig. 355 Left-side view of combat stances.

Fig. 356 From above the interaction is seen more clearly.

Fig. 357 Front view of 'attacked' figure's posture.

Fig. 358 The assailant is at the extent of his reach.

Figure Seven

This figure comes from the Dragon German Medical Troops set, which is quite old now, but none the worse for that. The chap with a headache, lying on a stretcher, will replicate a soldier who has just been shot several times by one of the tank riders. This conversion repeats a number of the techniques shown earlier in the chapter, but is a precis in subtlety. Fig. 359 shows the right and left leg components cut into their 'breakdown' positions. In Fig. 360, the top of the left leg is shown. The upper portion is bent using pliers so that the thigh will rise

slightly to accommodate the bend of the knee shown in Fig. 361. Fig. 362 shows the new head in place, along with a slight dent, which has been carved out with a scalpel. The dent will later be sanded with fine emery paper. The filling (Fig. 363) is minimal, and should be filed and carefully sanded to replace the clothing creases when dry. In Fig. 364 the arms find their final position. The right hand is representing the shocked state of the soldier, whilst the left hand is reaching for his neck wound. The finished figure is shown at Fig. 365, ready for his paint coat. Fig. 366 shows the final paint applied.

RIGHT: *Fig. 359
Components broken
down to basics.*

BELOW: *Fig. 360
The top of the left leg
part.*

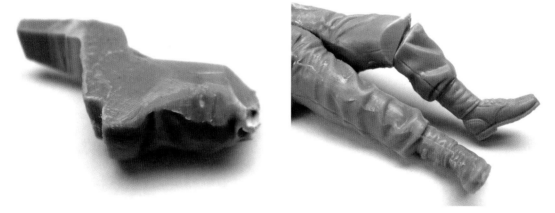

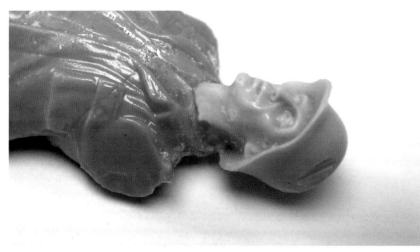

ABOVE: *Fig. 361
Bend induced to the
left knee.*

LEFT: *Fig. 362
Helmet dent added
with a craft knife
blade.*

127

RIGHT: *Fig. 363 Careful joint filling is required throughout construction.*

BELOW: *Fig. 364 Hand positioning is critical to the 'shocked' posture of the figure.*

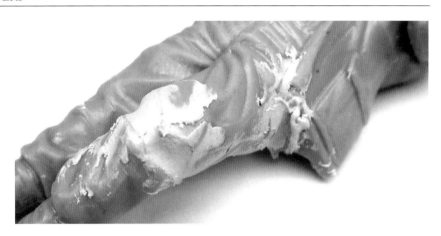

ABOVE: *Fig. 365 New creases are added with scalpel, file and emery paper.*

LEFT: *Fig. 366 The final painting of the figure.*

The Diorama

The arrangement of troops on this diorama took a significant amount of finalizing. I was also anxious to illustrate in these photographs how well the figures work in Fig. 367 and 368, where they are not in the originally envisaged positions shown in Figs. 369 to 371. Fig. 367 shows the first part of their patrol in the northern Leningrad sector, when an enemy position has been spotted. In Fig. 368, a snapshot from the time is replicated, as a German Stuka anti-tank aircraft squeals into

Fig. 367 Tank riders atop their KV5 on the Leningrad front.

Fig. 368 Stuka Panzerknacker attacks from the rear.

the attack. The figures are reacting realistically to the threat. Figs. 369 and 370 show two views of the finally selected figure positions during their engagement with the ground troops. The bitterness of the close-quarters battle which ensues in Fig. 371 is exemplified by the expression on the face of the Master Box German figure with the rifle and bayonet.

Fig. 369 The enemy is sighted and the tank riders disembark.

ABOVE: Fig. 370 The sniper's-eye view.

RIGHT: Fig. 371 Close-quarters combat was a feature of the Leningrad front.

WEAPON REFERENCE

Figs. 372, 373 and 374 in this section are provided so that an alternative to the kit weapons can be converted if desired. The weapon is a late-war PPSH sub-machine gun. Although it retains many of the external characteristics of the earlier PPSH-41, this was a much-improved weapon. It utilized many components copied from the Suomi m-1931, an excellent sub-machine gun

designed and built by disaffected Germans in Finland before the Second World War.

This is an extremely well-detailed and well-sculpted figure combination, which, thanks to modern mass-production methods, can be kept cost-effective. You can, of course, adapt these and similar figures to suit all tanks, as near to the war's end all combative nation's troops were carried in this way at one time or another.

Fig. 372 Russian PPSH sub-machine gun 1943.

Fig. 373 The weapon's breech detail.

Fig. 374 Magazine and entry port details.

CHAPTER 7

Cossack Dance

THE HISTORY

Throughout the latter stages of Operation 'Barbarossa' (Hitler's invasion of Russia), the German Army and Waffen SS units became seriously depleted. This was often as a result of simple attrition, but also as a consequence of the second front opening up in Europe in 1944. As a result, the SS in particular put together units of foreign nationals. Some were sympathetic to the Nazi cause, and some were simply prisoners of war, if not of conscience. The Cossack units of the SS (Schutzstaffel) were employed initially in southern Russia, and latterly in Yugoslavia and North-West Europe. With traditions dating back before the modern state of Russia even existed, the Cossacks were the Steppe warriors of legend. Leo Tolstoy's book *The Cossacks* and Gogol's *Taras Bulba* portray a group of drunken, comical, yet utterly fearless warrior brigands. The realities of a mechanized war changed their world for ever.

The Russian Army operated vast numbers of horse-mounted Cossack units throughout the war in Europe. By comparison, the German employment of such troops was relatively limited. The German Cossacks of the Don and Terek River, however, became feared throughout Russia and the Balkans for their ruthlessness, and lack of desire to give quarter in battle. I had originally envisaged this vignette (small diorama) as taking place in a tavern on the Russo-German border, as the retreating pro-German units were forced together in 'patch battalions', desperately trying to stem the tide of the Russian 'shock armies' of the late-war period. I finally settled upon a scene in the outdoors, as this gave me the opportunity to include some armoured vehicles, and portray more of the 'anxiousness' of the times.

CREATING THE MODEL

I scanned the pages of *Military Modelling* magazine for any clue to the availability of 1/35th Cossack figure kits. I noticed one or two single figures in resin, but none of them seemed particularly 'animated' in their postures. Russian model manufacturer Zvezda have had an excellent set of two such soldiers in their range for quite some years. They have recently been joined by a stunning set of four 'Soviet Cossacks' on horseback, which are exceptionally well animated and sculpted – their facial expressions are second to none. I

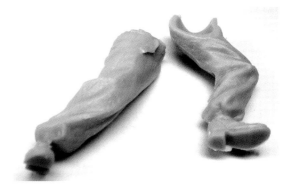

Fig. 375 First, select the most appropriate legs.

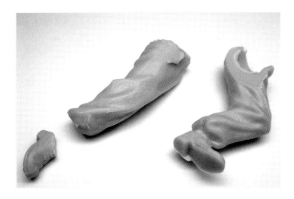

Fig. 376 Using a heavy craft blade, commence surgery.

Fig. 377 Assemble legs and align carefully.

took elements from the Zvezda kit, the now venerable DML 'German Cossack Cavalry' kit, and parts from 'German Tank Repair Crew' by Mini Art, in order to vary the positions and 'attitude' of the final dance troupe.

Figure One

Fig. 375 shows the legs selected from the 'German Tank Repair Crew'. They are parts 'D2' and 'E3'. These legs were chosen after viewing a DVD of the Russian State Cossack Troupe dancing on stage in Moscow, quickly employing the freeze-frame mode in order to gather any usable footage. It is a veritable blur of action when they dance! In Fig. 376, the

right foot is removed with a scalpel, and a triangular 2mm thick sliver of plastic carved away from the rear portion of the upper shoe, in order that it will point downwards when re-affixed to the bottom of the trouser leg. These legs might appear at odds with those with the longer boots of the DML Cossacks, but they are more in keeping with the late-war period, when leather was in short supply for German forces, even elite SS units. In Fig. 377 the legs are assembled, and feet added. Fig. 378 leads us to the waist area, where misalignment of the differential leg combination must be dealt with. With the leg assembly upturned, place the waist area against a piece of emery paper secured to

Fig. 378 Close-up view of the waist area.

Fig. 379 60-thou laminations of plastic sheet.

the table-top, and move back and forth until the waist is levelled. Once this step is complete, the waist will be 3–4mm shorter than when you began sanding.

Cut two 60-thou sheets of plastic card, and join them to the legs in the manner shown at Fig. 379, test-fitting the torso as you proceed. When set, sand the assembly, and re-introduce some of the creases lost in the previous process. Fig. 380 sees the model filler applied, which is gently sanded once the whole is set hard. Fig. 381shows assembly of the torso/head components – the former is from the DML Cossacks, whilst the latter comes from the Zvezda Cossack set. The facial features on the Zvezda item are beautifully rendered. The Russian star can easily be replaced with the German eagle at a later stage.

In Fig. 382 the figure begins to come to life, after another look at the dance DVD. The figure's left arm is taken from the DML figure's sprue, raised slightly from the kit's recommended position, once in place, as shown. The right arm is cannibalized from the Airfix Multipose set of British Infantry. These figures are in 1/32nd scale but, if used sensibly and with a little common sense, the mix in scales can be managed, and no one will be able

Fig. 380 Model filler must be carefully applied to entire area as shown.

Fig. 381 Torso and head choice is all-important.

Fig. 382 The shortened Multipose arm is now added.

to 'see the join'. It is a fact that some people have larger hands than others, but manufacturers tend to use an 'aggregate' size in their figure production. With Multipose figures, the difference is at most negligible and, more often, not there at all! The fingers are so beautifully rendered that they are often preferable to DML's counterparts, particularly on some of their earlier figures. As far as arm length is concerned, a 2mm sliver removed from the armpit end resulted in the perfect fit, and effect. Figs. 383 and 384 illustrate the figure sub-assemblies joined together momentarily with a tiny spot of glue, and the different viewpoints examined in order to see that the final product is convincing.

In Fig. 385, the 15-thou plastic sheet is being 'crimped'. Cut this to shape with a sharp scalpel, using the template provided. This will represent the Cossack's long coat as he whirls around in drunken ecstasy. It will come up higher the faster he spins, so choose the final height you prefer, before committing to your final figure stance. The crimping of 15-thou sheet is easy. During the process of adding undulations and folds (*see* picture), do not be afraid to pinch the plastic portions completely

Fig. 383 Carefully join the torso and leg assembly together in a test-fit.

Fig. 384 Check from all angles to ensure realism.

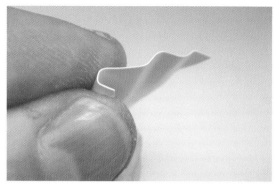

Fig. 385 Hand-crimp the shallow folds in the coat tails.

together as the sheet will not break. Unfortunately, the material has a lot of 'spring-back' inherent in it, and it may take several attempts before you get a satisfactory finish. Fig. 386 shows the coat-tails in place, glued securely to the waist portion, whilst Figs. 387 and 388 show different views of the figure with correctly aligned torso and legs. The model filler is applied to the shoulders and waist areas

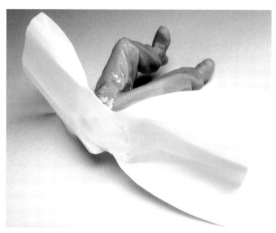

Fig. 386 Coat-tails test-fitted to leg assembly.

Fig. 387 Final assembly can now take place.

Fig. 388 Turn the assembly to check correct alignment of parts.

in Figs. 389 and 390, then sanded carefully with small pieces of progressively fine emery paper until the seams and creases are restored.

Figs. 391 and 392 are shots of the finished item with the addition of the DML figure's hood and tassles – the latter being used to warm and protect the face and neck areas during a long winter march.

Fig. 389 Carefully fill both of the shoulder joints where needed.

Fig. 390 Use model filler to pad out the waist area.

Fig. 391 Attach the relevant hood and tassles.

Fig. 392 Final check from low angle left.

*Fig. 393 Paint applied
(view from front left).*

*Fig. 394 The realism of
his stance is critical.
Dancing puts the body
deliberately off balance!*

Figure Two

This figure represents the epitome of the Cossack dancer, crouched and kicking, his arms coming up to a folded position. The principal components for this conversion all come from the 'German Tank Repair Crew' from Mini Art, as their baggy shirts and pants well represent the more traditional form of Cossack uniform, first formalized in the 15th century.

Fig. 395 shows the choice of legs ('B2' and 'A3'), from the kit. The boots need to be severed and adjusted to the attitude shown in Fig. 396, once the mould-lines and sprue remains have been carefully trimmed away. Fig. 397 shows the torso, 'A3' from the instruction sheet, glued in place on the leg assembly. A little packing with model filler will need to take place at the left, lower waist, but it is minimal, so do not miss it! At Fig. 398 the base has been added (40-thou sheet). Make sure when adding the base that it is glued at the point relative to the figure that will impart maximum stability to the finished item. Fig. 399 sees the upper portion of part 'A5' (with the forearm removed), fixed in place at the left shoulder of the figure. Angle the elbow portion slightly to make sure that the forearm from component

Fig. 395 Selected legs glued in place together.

Fig. 396 Repositioning of feet into a 'dance' attitude.

Fig. 397 Selection of the most appropriate torso is necessary.

Fig. 398 A base is fabricated from 20-thou plastic sheet.

139

Fig. 399 Upper left arm selection and joint.

Fig. 400 Left forearm is added from a different arm type.

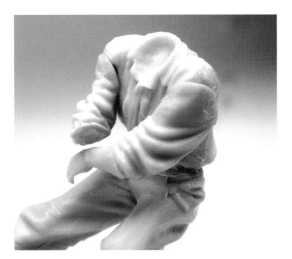

Fig. 401 Right upper arm is added next.

Fig. 402 Right forearm sits in place to replicate arms in the process of folding.

'C5' will fit, once it has been removed from the arm (Fig. 400). Fig. 401 shows the position of the right upper arm ('A4') relative to the body. The elbow has been chamfered and angled prior to the addition of the forearm taken from part 'C4'.

Fig. 403 shows the semi-dry run, to test the fit before final glueing and trimming takes place. The great thing about this stage is that any mis-alignment can be cured, and the figure components adjusted, before the model-glue sets. Figs. 404 and 405 illustrate well the need to choose a head carefully. Refer to any reference pictures you may have, to ensure that you choose well, and that all of the components complement and harmonize with each other throughout the process. In Figs. 406 and 407, the figure is checked for authenticity of posture.

Fig. 403 Test-fit all components first, before glueing in place.

Fig. 404 Choose a head that will provide a face with the most apt expression.

Fig. 405 Head shown in place on neck/torso.

Fig. 406 Check the stance throughout from all angles.

ABOVE: *Fig. 407 Final assembly viewed from rear left.*

RIGHT: *Fig. 408 Paint is applied via airbrush and conventional paintbrushes.*

Figure Three

The balalaika was the Cossack musician's accessory of choice. This traditional Russian and Eastern European instrument's origins were as old and venerable as the Cossack brotherhood itself, with individual balalaikas changing hands, even during wartime, for vast sums of money.

Fig. 409 begins the story – the 'German Machine Gun Crew on Manoeuvers' from Tamiya provides the legs for this figure. Parts 'A1' and 'A4' are assembled as per the kit instructions, making sure that the feet marry exactly, and the waist is level, when placed on a flat surface. Fig. 410 shows the addition of the other torso from the DML 'Cossack Cavalry' set, making sure to align the two in the manner shown (with a bias of twist at the waist, to the left). Fig. 411 shows the correct waist position,

Fig. 409 Legs are chosen from the Tamiya range.

Fig. 410 Ensure exact alignment of the waist joint.

and a little filling with model-glue – for fine gaps, model filler is not always necessary. Fig. 412 shows the choice of the Cossack head with the open mouth from the Zvezda kit – note the 3 different colours of plastic! The arms are added next (Figs. 413 and 414); as they are from the Airfix Multipose range, a little trimming to the arm's length is in order, as on the first figure.

At this point, the balalaika should be fabricated, from plastic-sheet laminations, then added, along with the right arm, as in Fig. 414. The glue will not be set as yet, and the whole arm/instrument assembly can be twisted slightly until the optimum position for all of the elements is discovered.

Four different colours of manufacturer's body parts are seen in Fig. 415; at the painting stage, they will all merge seamlessly, providing you sand the joints where necessary.

Fig. 411 Carefully fill smaller gaps with model-glue.

Fig. 412 The excellent Zvezda Cossack head in place.

Fig. 413 A suitably altered Multipose arm in place.

Fig. 414 The balalaika is hewn from plastic sheet components.

Fig. 415 The range of different-coloured plastics is now evident.

Fig. 416 Finished figure after painting.

Figure Four

The fourth figure is by far the simplest of the soldiers to convert. The gentleman depicted is from the SS Handschar division, which was formed from pre-war Fascist extremists in Croatia. Although fanatical and skilled fighters (in the mountains and the lowlands), they were to be used, unwittingly, as cannon-fodder by the main SS units, who really considered them *Untermenschen* (in other words, not of Aryan extraction) and therefore little better than sub-human.

Fig. 417 shows the leg jointing of this figure, which is not a great deal different overall from that of the basic chap in the packet. He is, in fact, figure 'B' from the DML 'Panzergrenadier Division Grossdeutschland' kit. In Fig. 418 the upper torso is added, after all mould-lines have been carefully removed with a fresh scalpel blade. The right arm is removed (Fig. 419), to be replaced with a new 'bionic' hand from the Hornet range. At Fig. 420 the left hand is removed, and twisted slightly inwards (Fig. 421). Fig. 422 illustrates the exceptional quality of the hands available in the Hornet range. In Fig. 423, the right hand has been selected, along with a suitably open-mouthed Croatian head (with fez), from 'HGH 2-5 Heads Wearing Fez', also from the Hornet range.

ABOVE: *Fig. 417 Carefully adjusted leg joints are critical.*

RIGHT: *Fig. 418 Add torso with correct degree of lateral twist.*

Fig. 419 Replace the figure's hand with a suitable Hornet type.

Fig. 420 The angle at which you cut the wrist is important.

Fig. 421 Final arm positions now checked.

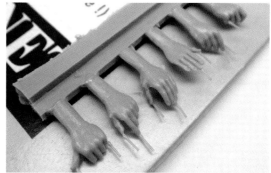

Fig. 422 New hands in resin, from Hornet.

Fig. 423 The final selection of Hornet components.

In Figs. 424 and 425, the new hand and head are in place. These are fixed using cyanoacrylate adhesive (super-glue) and accelerator. First, place a small blob of the glue on the neck portion on top of the torso. Place the head, with the neck cut at the chosen angle, on to the glue, and wait a few minutes for it to begin to set. Likewise, glue the hand on to the wrist stub and cement it in place. If you use super-glue 'gel', the hand will stick sufficiently on contact for you to spray on the activator, so setting the whole assembly instantly. Fig. 426 shows the incredible detail of the right hand, with the fingernail clearly visible on the centre finger; such components can bring great credibility to a figure model.

Fig. 424 Final assembly of all parts.

Fig. 425 Check finished figure from all angles.

ABOVE: *Fig. 426 Close-up of hand details.*

RIGHT: *Fig. 427 The figure in action and painted.*

The foreign nationals that fought for the Germans during the Second World War came from countries with great warrior traditions, most of whom now co-exist in great harmony. Their contributions to the rich tapestry of the history of 'Europa' should not be under-estimated. This was a very interesting diorama to research, resulting in an interesting diversion from tanks and guns.

DIORAMA FURTHER REFERENCE

RIGHT: *Fig. 428 Handschar figure leans into the scene.*

BELOW: *Fig. 429 The whirling posture of the figure is enhanced by the position of the coat-tails.*

ABOVE: *Fig. 430 The balalaika player is walking towards the dancers.*

LEFT: *Fig. 431 The attention to such details as the coat's hood is all-important.*

RIGHT: *Fig. 432 The band and dancers should appear as though moving in harmony.*

BELOW: *Fig. 433 An excellent way to forget your troubles!*

CHAPTER 8

Band of Brothers – Out of Ammo

THE HISTORY

The American 101st Airborne troops of the Second World War were among the finest soldiers of any army at that time. Their counterparts in the German order of battle were also feared and respected throughout the world, being the inventors of modern airborne warfare. This 'band of brothers', immortalized in the TV series of the same name, were trained in the USA and the UK, to help spearhead the invasion of North-West Europe on the eve of D-Day. The diorama depicts a moment during the week following 6 June, when Allied forces were combining in order to push inland. The US forces were pitted against all sorts of patch units made up of troops from all over Normandy. The German Paras in the Normandy sector were told that they would, for the first time since their mauling on Crete, be fighting after an airborne landing. Unfortunately for them, there were no Junkers Ju 52s available for any sort of sortie behind the allied lines, and they were finally committed to battle as infantry.

CREATING THE MODEL

The DML figures for this conversion were chosen on the basis that they are the best figures for the job. I planned the diorama knowing that these very cost-effective model kits could be converted to interact well together – and also they remain the only ones available, unless you can stretch to the slightly more expensive, yet equally excellent, resin models. You can, of course, convert resin model figures, and mix and match parts from both types of kit. It is an indisputable fact that, however many figures there are available, you will often need to convert one or more to arrive at exactly the era or stance that you require for a particular situation.

Figure One

Very often the sculptural quality and exact stance of a figure does not match that of the box artwork as precisely as the purchaser might hope. Fortunately in the case of DML's 'US Screaming Eagle – Normandy 1944', minimal changes are necessary to remedy this situation.

Figs. 434 and 435 show the first step. After carefully removing the torso/leg assembly halves from the sprue, glue them together in the manner shown, taking great care to align the legs and body sides as exactly as possible, before

Fig. 434 Masking tape ensures a closed joint for glueing.

Fig. 435 Careful alignment reduces trimming.

taping in place until set. Doing this will pay dividends when trimming, filling and sanding the joints, which will automatically be minimal. Figs. 436 and 437 illustrate the need to check the figure from every angle throughout construction to achieve a convincing stance. Once the boots are in place, Fig. 438 shows how well the stance is progressing when the boots are

Fig. 436 Separate boots now in place.

Fig. 437 Check for correct stance before glue sets.

Fig. 438 Check position of boots on a flat surface.

Fig. 439 The arm is replaced with one from the DML 'Red Devil' kit.

Fig. 440 Use the jigsaw slowly and steadily.

ABOVE: *Fig. 441 Hinge the elbow joint once the slot is cut.*

RIGHT: *Fig. 443 Final model filler application to elbow joint.*

placed at an angle that helps the figure to balance – check the angle at which your own feet best support you when adopting the position of the final model. When glueing the boots in place, let them set for several minutes before placing the assembly on a flat surface (or in position on the diorama), with the feet on the ground. The soles of the boots on the flat surface will allow you to assess the most realistic body position relative to the legs. Then, you can let the whole thing dry in this position.

In order to achieve the more 'aggressive' stance shown in the box artwork, the left arm needs to be replaced – in this case with one from the DML 'British Airborne Red Devil, Arnhem 1944', shown in Fig. 439. Figs. 440, 441 and 442 show the arm's progression. In Fig. 440, the fine-pitched jigsaw blade is allowed to make its way through the elbow joint. Going from the 'crook' of the elbow outwards (and slowly)

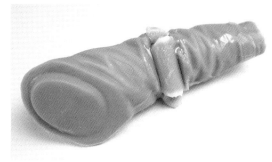

Fig. 442 Pack the joint with plastic strip slivers.

Fig. 444 'Red Devil' head halves selected.

ensures that the elbow can be hinged, as shown in Fig. 441. Fig. 442 shows the gap filled with plastic section cut from the kit's sprue. This will take time to set before the excess is trimmed, and the filler is added (Fig. 443). In the final assembly, the clothing creases have been filed back in place, paying particular attention to the forearm area, which is now almost flat.

Attention then turns to the head/neck area. The original kit head is quite scary, and not in a good way! I find it lacking in detail, and, contrary to what you might have been led to believe, no amount of excellent painting can make up for 'questionable' sculpting. It is replaced by the excellent British 'Para' head from the donor kit. Fig. 444 shows the front and rear head halves after the strap moulding has been trimmed away. Be sure to clean up any cut marks with fine emery paper until satisfactory. Figs. 445 and 446 show the head assembled, and the joint sanded and integrated, with a fine layer of model-glue 'wiped' on. In Fig. 447 the 'neck gap' is evident. Glue should only be applied once the neck area has been filled. Fig. 448 shows the neck, and the dreadful moulding of the original head (at right of picture). In Fig. 449 the neck is in place; a blob of filler has been applied to the base of the head before glueing it in place within the collar. This way, the neck will fill in properly, obviating the

Fig. 445 Head assembly carefully completed.

Fig. 446 Sand the joint carefully with fine emery paper.

Fig. 447 Neck joint requires filler before head is put into place.

Fig. 448 Comparison with original kit head provided.

Fig. 449 Final application of filler to outer neck portion.

Fig. 450 Test-fit rifle and adjust arm positions whilst glue is curing.

usual gap found when filling in the usual way – from outside after the head is in place.

Fig. 450 shows the improved stance of the figure. Once the arms are glued in the correct place, the hands are added, and the whole thing is allowed to dry for 10 minutes (depending on temperature and humidity), so that the joints hold but are still easy to manipulate. Add the M1 Garand rifle, and move the hands and arms until you achieve the most realistic position. Let the assembly set before removing the rifle to paint as a sub-assembly. Figs. 451 and 452 are the result of checking the final position and stance of the model. Any extra filling and sanding should take place at this stage. Fig. 453

Fig. 451 Check stance throughout assembly process.

Fig. 452 Use model filler if and where needed.

illustrates the final stage of filling, and the sanding and filing of the neck in-fill. Once the figure is complete, a thin coating of model-glue will help smooth the surface and ensure a good key for painting.

The Helmet

Fig. 454 shows the helmet (conspicuous by its absence from the original kit), which comes attached to the head in the 'US Marine Corps in the Korean War' 1/16th figure kit from the excellent 'Legend' company of Korea. Fig. 455 shows the first step in the removal of the face/cap-comforter portion, achieved by the steady use of a jigsaw and vice. Fig. 456 shows the beginning of the hollowing and edge-trimming. In Fig. 457, the drilling has begun in earnest (the vice has been omitted for clarity). At this stage, a hand-held miniature drill is best, with as large a drill-bit as the chuck will hold. With the helmet secured in the vice, drill until

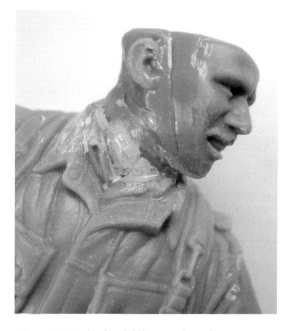

Fig. 453 Neck's final filling and sanding.

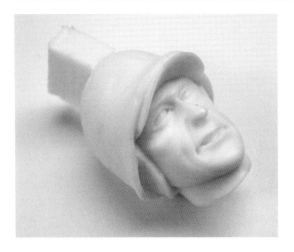

Fig. 454 Select the most appropriate donor head.

Fig. 455 Remove the face with a jigsaw.

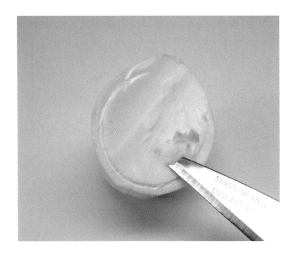

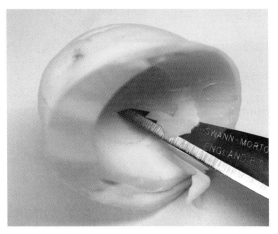

ABOVE LEFT: *Fig. 456 Begin the hollowing process with a craft blade.*

ABOVE RIGHT: *Fig. 457 Hollow out the helmet finally with a twist-drill.*

LEFT: *Fig. 458 Hollowing now completed.*

Fig. 459 Right side of face shown during painting.

Fig. 460 Left side of upper torso from the rear.

about half-way into the centre portion, then gently angle the bit, until the hole begins to open out at the edges (Fig. 458).

There are many US Forces 1/16th scale kits in resin from which you could choose a helmet. Try to choose a kit that will most relevantly fill your spares box!

Figure Two

Assessing Context

The second figure is the Falschirmjager trooper. He is reacting to the American who has crept up on him in the diorama, and as such requires a little more 'surgery'. How would you behave in a situation such as the one you are creating? Check references, and watch as much relevant footage from archive sources as possible. The German has been firing an MG 42, with a cyclic rate of fire in excess of 1,000 rounds per minute. As a result of being so close to this very loud weapon, he is momentarily partially deaf. (This weapon was not only loud, it was also much respected. In one incident in North-West Europe, a ceasefire was called by the British in order that the Germans could retrieve one that had been dropped, still firing, in the middle of a French street.) As the trooper turns to the American, he grabs his Sturmgewehr 44. Finding it empty, he waves it threateningly whilst reaching for a magazine of ammo. The US trooper likewise has no ammunition, and hopes that his bayonet will be enough.

Working on the Figure

This DML Falschirmjager figure is a little different from the norm, in as much as the arms and upper torso are an integral, two-piece moulding. As with the first figure, the mould quality is stunning, yet careful alignment of the halves and restraint with masking tape whilst the glue sets are required, in order to minimize trimming and joint integration. This stage, along with the legs, is covered by Figs. 461 and 462, whilst the head is seen in Fig. 463. It is an impressive piece once it has been assembled, and bears perhaps more than a passing resemblance to Prince Philip, the Duke of Edinburgh, a decorated ex-serviceman from the Second World War.

ABOVE: *Fig. 461 Body halves shown before arms are removed.*

RIGHT: *Fig. 462 Leg halves assembled and carefully aligned.*

BELOW: *Fig. 463 Head front and rear glued in place.*

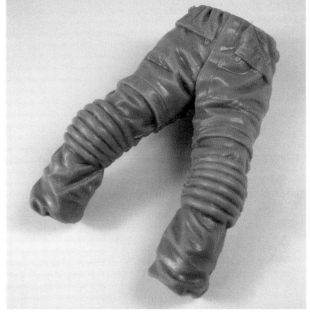

Severing the arms is the next step. (Of course, your models do not complain when they are undergoing such surgery, but during amputation of his shattered leg after Waterloo, the Earl of Uxbridge is reputed to have stopped the surgeon part way through the sawing to suggest that he get a new saw, as the one he was using was 'terribly blunt'! This remarkably resilient soldier also became the inventor of the first false limb.) Fig. 464 shows the ideal cut position, running along the shoulder seam of the tunic, or parachute smock. Seen from the front in Fig. 465, the cut is made slowly, whilst checking that the blade's progress is correct after each third stroke. The kit's severed left arm is consigned to the spares box, and is replaced with the spare left arm from the US 'Para' kit, after its shoulder joint plug has been filed off flush with the shoulder seam (Fig. 466). In Fig. 467, the right arm socket is shown with the burrs (from the sawing stage) having been trimmed and sanded away, ready to receive the

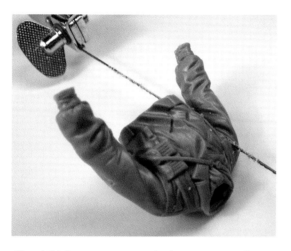

Fig. 464 Seam cutting with the assistance of a fine jigsaw blade.

Fig. 465 Slowly and carefully, always checking cut from all angles.

Fig. 466 US Airborne left arm is added.

Fig. 467 Preparation of the right arm joint.

amended right arm from the kit. Fig. 468 shows the portion of the arm's top that needs to be cut away (7mm in length), in order that the arm can be outstretched. In Fig. 469 the portion cut from the top of the redundant left arm is shown at the top right of the picture. This is grafted on to the top of the right arm (*see* Fig. 470), where the upper left arm is reversed, before being glued firmly into place. The model filler is added next (Fig. 471), and the whole thing is sanded and trimmed to remove the mould-lines and excess filler.

In Fig. 472 the now outstretched arm is glued in place at the shoulder joint. In Fig. 473,

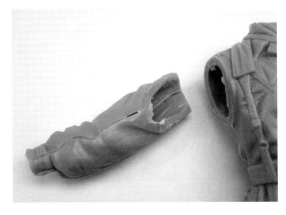

Fig. 468 Attitude of right arm outstretched.

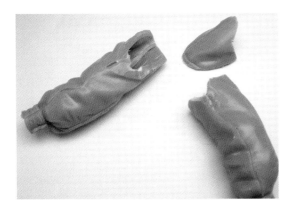

Fig. 469 Grafting portion of arm shown.

Fig. 470 The right arm is now complete and ready to fill.

Fig. 471 Carefully and sparingly, add the required amount of filler.

Fig. 472 The right arm is now joined to the torso.

Fig. 473 Fill the area around and inside the armpit area.

Fig. 474 Apply the model filler in thinner layers to aid the curing process.

the armpit area is filled, and the assembly is allowed to set hard. As a precaution, and to make application of this particular model filler much more easy, it is often preferable to let the filler set for several minutes after it has left the tube. This makes it less runny and more controllable on the scalpel blade, or toothpick applicator. Fig. 474 shows the second stage of

filling. You will find that thinner coats of filler dry more quickly and that this is preferable to piling it on. Three coats may seem tedious but this method will ensure that the filled area sets thoroughly. At Fig. 475, the arm's position is assessed for realism, whilst Fig. 476 shows the smoothing effect of a thin layer of model cement, which blends the filler and plastic

Fig. 475 Ensure throughout the assembly process that all parts are correctly aligned.

Fig. 476 Carefully blend the surface of the filler with model-glue.

Fig. 477 Underarm creases built up in layers.

Fig. 478 Final sanding of upper arm portion.

ABOVE: *Fig. 479 Creation of new seam around shoulder joint.*

RIGHT: *Fig. 480 New stance is now radically different to the kit position.*

perfectly after sanding with fine emery paper. Fig. 477 illustrates the way to build up the stretch marks in the underarm area. Scan your references, or ask a friend to hold out their arm whilst you take note of the creases in their sleeve, and how those creases change during the arm's movements.

The final sanding/blending in Fig. 478 is achieved by the careful use of emery paper, whilst the creases are best defined using a half-round mouse-tail file. Fig. 479 shows a small but critical stage in the reintegration of the right arm – using a mouse-tail file and emery paper to define the shoulder seam. In Fig. 480, the trooper grabs the ammunition clip, which has previously been cut from the Sturmgewehr 44.

Fig. 481 The finished paratrooper in a posture of defence.

US 101ST REFERENCE

The United States of America entered the Second World War with no airborne infantry forces at her disposal. Once they were organized, and mobilized, they became a formidable fighting unit, immortalized in the TV series *Band of Brothers*. The 101st Airborne, or 'Screamin' Eagles', are now the benchmark against which other similar units are judged, and re-enactments of their wartime exploits are a critical component of 'wartime weekends' across Europe, Great Britain and North America.

Our model for this reference shoot is the redoubtable Airborne Forces expert, Ian 'Bombo' Bailey, who very kindly agreed to let me take the accompanying reference photographs of him wearing his later-pattern Airborne combat uniform (some of it 60-plus years old), in order to provide extra information for super-dctailers, and those who may prefer something a little more major in the way of 'surgery'.

Fig. 485 shows him in typical garb for 'D plus 5' onwards, when the fighting equipment of the paratrooper had been 'refined' for use in the field, any extraneous equipment having been ditched. Fig. 486 illustrates the

Fig. 482 US equipment detail showing similarity to Ranger uniform. (Illustration by the author.)

ABOVE: *Fig. 483 German Falschirmjager parachute assault badge.* (Courtesy of James Waters' collection.)

RIGHT: *Fig. 484 The paratrooper camouflage smock as used in NW Europe.* (Illustration by the author.)

importance of insignia in the field. The helmet markings are in white, yet they are understated and subdued beneath the helmet netting. The dyed-green leather patch pockets on the 'jump' trousers (Fig. 487) are quite stiff, and appear to 'sit' quite differently if filled with ammunition, as depicted on Dragon's model. The uniform rear shot (Fig. 488) shows the slight difference in shade of green between trousers and tunic. Military clothing was produced in various parts

Fig. 485 Paratrooper Ian Bailey during a lull in the fighting.

of the US at different times throughout the war, with different dyes in different combinations, all mixed up together and issued to millions of men and women – inevitably, the perfect matching of colours remains elusive! Figs. 489, 490 and 491 show the kneeling/firing stance from various angles. Of particular interest here is the diffused light from a relatively overcast sky, which gives a perfect idea of exactly where the shadows under the clothing creases should be

Fig. 486 Useful stance for foot patrol.

Fig. 487 Standard late-issue uniform front.

Fig. 489 Kneeling and firing posture right rear.

ABOVE: *Fig. 488 Uniform rear view. Note position of pistol holster.*

painted, and the general feel of a standard figure's overall look after painting. This, of course, is applicable in any scale. In Fig. 492, the clothing creases are completely different, and more exaggerated around the legs and arms.

Fig. 493 shows the 'verdigris', or copper/brass discolouration on the canteen press-studs, which would occur very quickly in wet field conditions. In Fig. 494 the extra ammo pouch

Fig. 490 Left front view of firing posture.

ABOVE: *Fig. 491 front view of aiming/firing posture.*

LEFT: *Fig. 492 Seated in his Jeep, Ian carefully marks his target.*

Fig. 493 Canteen canvas and stud detail.

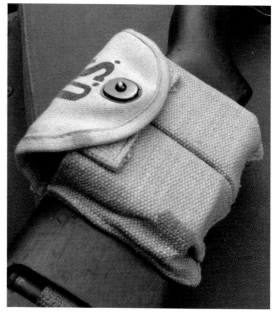

Fig. 494 Canvas cover for .30 calibre rounds.

(of canvas construction) is seen attached to the butt of the carbine. In Fig. 495, there is a definite case for a dry-brushing application! The entrenching tool's canvas cover became scuffed very quickly in the field. This genuine Second

World War item has actually survived relatively well; the stitching in Fig. 63 is testament to that. The rear of the holster for the 1911-pattern Colt .45 calibre pistol is shown in Fig. 497. The rear face of these items represented a fine

Fig. 495 The entrenching tool cover is original Second World War issue.

ABOVE: *Fig. 496 The stitching and stud detail of the entrenching tool cover.*

RIGHT: *Fig. 497 An unusual view of the pistol holster rear detail.*

example of the leatherman's art. In Fig. 498, Ian has adopted the classic 'Weaver' stance. In order to achieve more accuracy, over a longer range, he is bracing his right arm against the barn's wall. His 'Screamin' Eagle' insignia has been stitched on with olive drab twine, which was issued to troops in the field in order that they could mend slight tears in their uniform, and darn their socks during long periods away from the Quartermaster's store.

Fig. 498 Ian adopts Sheriff Weaver's 'bracing stance'.

DIORAMA REFERENCE

Fig. 499 The assailants face to face.

ABOVE LEFT: *Fig. 500 They are both out of ammunition.*

ABOVE: *Fig. 501 The autumn camouflage pattern.*

LEFT: *Fig. 502 The 'Screamin' Eagle' patch is clearly visible on the US figure's upper left arm.*

ABOVE: *Fig. 503 It is important to assess your figure's interaction from all angles.*

RIGHT: *Fig. 504 The diorama wall is constructed using proprietary embossed plastic sheet.*

Index